Liquid
LOVE

A JOURNEY THROUGH LIFE'S CONTRADICTIONS

DR. RENA' D. MORROW

ISBN 978-1-0980-4114-4 (paperback)
ISBN 978-1-0980-4115-1 (digital)

Christian Faith Publishing, Inc.
832 Park Avenue
Meadville, PA 16335
www.christianfaithpublishing.com

Printed in the United States of America

FOREWORD

This is one of the most remarkable books I have read in my life. That, in itself, is a rather significant declaration, considering the fact that I have read in excess of one thousand books in about four decades of a totally exciting literary adventure. Quite beyond simply reading another book, however, what makes the author's work singularly appealing to the more discerning aspect of my persona is that, in the first instance, she speaks a language that is simply one that I speak each day of my life. That language is one of unconditional love. It is also a language of the combined philosophy of the Excellent Triad of Faith, Love, and Hope. In the third instance, the author's divinely-inspired concept of *Liquid Love* has found invaluable utility and purpose in my own spiritual life and practice. As an ardent practitioner of spiritual meditation, these days, I derive sheer intoxicating pleasure from slipping easily and tranquilly into God's awesome presence simply by imagining a current of golden and viscous liquid love coursing through my entire being! Finally, of true and ultimate significance, it is a language of total trust in the eternal loving wisdom of the Divine.

I would be guilty of grave negligence if I failed to acknowledge that the author expresses herself with such lucidity and fluidity of thought that I am left gasping at the sheer creative genius that the Divine can bring forth in His creatures whenever He is ready to impart certain immutable truths to mankind. As I read this book, I was continually assailed by the distinct feeling that I was reading from a mind that is as clean as a glass of clear spring water. I realized I was in the awesome presence of a mind, and a soul, that had been subjected to unspeakable previous trauma but which had, in all likelihood, and by a conscious act of willpower, sought authentic succor and rest in the healing power that is embedded in our faithful search for our gracious Lord's unfailing and unconditional love.

The beauty of this search is that it invariably leads us to the place where we discover love, compassion, and empathy for ourselves and for others. One of the sublime dividends of arrival at a place of loving healing is that our mind, having shed the burden of dysfunctionality, anger, vengeance, resentment, and self-loathing, it is now left beautifully clear for the germination of creative seeds, very much like the fertile farm ground that has been cleared of useless weed and is now ready to receive the farmer's seedlings for the cultivation of healthy produce. That was the sort of creative mind I encountered on the pages you are about to read.

It is an inescapable truth that most of us have passed through, or will pass through, a great deal of heartache and pain on this life journey. Most of such heart-wrenching and painful events are ones that we would wish had never occurred. For us to cultivate the mindset that will accord us a life of peace and joy, we will require the ability to view our very existence from a broader perspective and extract what lessons we can glean from it. It is from this oasis of perception that we can then proceed to create a more meaningful life for ourselves and for others, especially our loved ones.

Life is a truly magical project. In all essence, that project is actually a spiritual journey whose path is strewn with the priceless gems that have been placed at certain strategic locations with an obligation for us to unearth them. Gold, for instance, is a treasure that, for millennia, man has labored to dig deep into the bowels of the earth to reach. In fact, it is documented that the earliest gold mine may be as old as seven thousand years. Fascinatingly, there is another type of gold. This is the gold in every human experience, seemingly good or seemingly bad. Indeed and in fact, there is gold in even the most difficult and the most horrendous of experiences. To extract riches from these experiences and by natural extension, our life, all we need to do is find the gold therein. As we dig, it is merely a point of fact that we will finally discover nuggets of gold in the form of truths and lessons that we will use to heal our hurts and anger, and as this happens, we should make it a point to cherish these experiences and be grateful for them. Therein lie the invaluable dividends of unearthing the real treasures that will enrich our soul and the souls of others when they hear our stories.

How we choose to view our life story and those events in it that eventually mold us into who we ultimately become will either be invaluable instruments for our empowerment or they will keep us stranded in the past, possibly riddled with regret and resentment. In sober truth, our life story is possibly the best gift that our Lord could give us. To justify this gift, all we need to do is embrace our past agonies as necessary ingredients for growth in our love walk with God. That is how we will ultimately connect with our true life purpose. Our story is akin to that of the rough and brittle piece of rock by the seaside that is subjected to years of sustained friction by the elements until it finally becomes a smooth and beautiful pebble.

Finally, I sincerely commend this book to you. It is one of the most spiritually inspiring works I have had the privilege of reading. It is a book of simple utility in its delivery of not only life changing, but in certain critical situations, life-saving nuggets of wisdom. Additionally, the author has not only presented her work in such a way as to make for infinitely easy reading, assimilation, and application. The book is also one finished in exquisite literary taste. Happy reading.

Dr. Yomi Garnett, Ambassador
Philadelphia, Pennsylvania
March 2019

INTRODUCTION

*There is no fear in love. But perfect love drives out
fear, because fear has to do with punishment. The
one who fears is not made perfect in love.*
                                    —1 John 4:18 (NIV)

It must have been merely a question of perfect Divine timing that I
found myself quietly sitting on the pier of Chesapeake Bay on that mild
summer day of 2018. Chesapeake Bay is an estuary that extends through
the states of Maryland, Delaware, District of Columbia and Virginia. I
was at the premises of Sandy Cove Ministries, an all-inclusive, all year-
round Christian retreat center located on the headwaters of Chesapeake
Bay in North East Maryland. Like many other people, I had come to
Sandy Cove Christian Center in anticipation of a special time away with
God. In retrospect, I can't help feeling that I was on that pier at that
particular time, and on that particular day, for the particular reason that
I was scheduled for a visitation from God. As the moist wind from the
waters of the estuary blew across my face, so did a barely audible voice
whisper a question into my ears. At first, I thought it was the soft howl
of the wind but pricked up my ears to be sure. I heard the voice again. It
was little above a whisper yet distinct enough to be heard.

"Where have you been?"

My mind immediately went to Moses's encounter with God
on the holy ground on Mount Sinai, more than four thousand years
ago. Instantly, with a feeling of total awe and wonder, I knew that I
had just heard a word from Him. I also knew instinctively that the
question was a rhetorical question from the very heart of God.

At that surreal moment, a few thoughts ran through my mind:

"Why had I been chosen for this visitation?"

"What was the real purpose of this encounter?"

"What was the meaning of the question?"

"How was I supposed to respond to the question?"

Very quickly, however, I recovered my wits and realized that all I needed to immediately do was simply reflect the question back to myself, and that was what I did.

"Rena', where have you been?"

Better still, "Where exactly are you coming from?"

At that moment of soul-searching, my need for an answer, being as urgent as it was important, I felt my mind go into a calm repose, even as I knew with a certain knowing that the Holy Spirit, the all-wise Counselor, would come to my aid. I was not disappointed.

The memories came flooding back. They were memories of a traumatic and tumultuous past and ones that seemed to have threatened my very existence as a Christian. They were memories of experiences that attempted to destroy my love for others and my trust in them. They were memories that threatened to dash my hope for a certain glorious future against an unyielding rock of total despair.

Accepting all these thoughts as being perfectly true, I asked myself the next logical question:

"So what do all these really mean in my life?"

The answer came in an insightful revelation as the rivulets of tears cascaded down my cheeks.

"You have been stuck in a state of rejection. You have wallowed for too long in a place of hurt. Anger has eaten and is still eating away at your soul. The spirit of lack of forgiveness has taken residence in the wonderful space that compassionate understanding, charity, and humane accommodation should be occupying. Because of all these, you have turned a cold shoulder toward God. And since your face is turned away from Him, He finds it difficult to locate your face."

With my heart thumping furiously within my chest, I choked back the tears as I said audibly, "Yes, this is all so true, Lord. Forgive me. Here I am. Heal me. The place I am coming from does not glorify you. I am ready to receive the soothing balm of your love."

At that moment, a gust of wind blew across my face on that scenic pier, and in that wind was the caressing hand of God. In that gust

of wind was an incomparable warmth—the warmth of His unconditional love. In that gust of wind was the divine caress in which I
felt nothing but the gentleness of His love. In that soft yet powerful
wind, I felt the awesome and totally forgiving power of His love. And
then, at that moment, I felt as if a liquid current of ethereal energy
was flowing down my entire body, from the top of my scalp to the
toes of my feet. It was a sensation like none I had ever experienced in
my life. At that moment, I arrived at the ultimate revelation of the
authentic nature of God's total, unconditional, and uncompromising
love.

This was love in action.

This was liquid love!

In that instant of revelation, all my fears dissolved, and I came
into a perfect understanding of the scripture in 1 John chapter 4,
verse 18 (NIV): "There is no fear in love. But perfect love drives out
fear, because fear has to do with punishment. The one who fears is
not made perfect in love." Indeed, all my fears were dissolved into a
nothingness, and on that day, my heart melted into the soft and yielding mass of the liquid love of God. And in my total acceptance of
His will and love, God wrapped His hands around my cold heart and
squeezed, and the liquid love came pouring out of my very essence.
God had, in His absolute benevolence, taken me back to love. Little
wonder He said in 1 Corinthians chapter 13 and verse 13 (NIV),
"And now these three remain: faith, hope and love. But the greatest
of these is love." Yes, the greatest of all is love, and nothing but love.

At this moment, all fear had left me. God had melted my heart
today with his liquid love. Yes, God has, and will always take me back
to love, for "the greatest of these is love," He said. Yes, my impres-
sion at this moment is that I have been fighting to get my surrender
back. All that love and the many sacrifices I made for them had been
misused and abused over and over again. Yes, I wanted my surrender
back because I didn't want them to hurt me anymore. But at that
moment, when God touched my heart, He made me to understand
that for me to get my surrender back from those who had hurt me
was also to ask for my surrender back from God Himself. But along
the way, the pains of distrust and mistrust had robbed me of that

surrender as I fought to take my 'surrender' back. In essence, I had been fighting for my life. But on this beautiful day on Chesapeake Bay, God reminded me, as it says in the scripture of Matthew chapter 16 and verse 25 (NIV), "For whoever wants to save their life will lose it, but whoever loses their life for me will find it." What a powerful truth this had become for me! For I had willingly agreed to lose my life of pain, distrust, mistrust, and agony, and now I could gloriously reclaim my new life of surrender.

I found myself contrasting these powerful words of God with those in the devil's "bible," in which it seemingly and untruthfully declares, "You have a right to live your life anyway you want to." However, wouldn't anyone with the least bit of common sense agree that living one's life in just about any way one chooses can be ultimately detrimental to one's life, and that of others, especially loved ones? Such a pattern of life can only take one on the path of destructive mistrust. Most certainly, no relationship can endure or be healthy when it is built on distrust.

With these thoughts, I was ushered into my new place of intimacy with God, and it is a place that completely recognizes that the effects of distrust are illicit and secret living, selfish, and self-centered decisions, the concealing of information, the playing of unwholesome games, the manipulation of the affections of a loved one, false and prideful bravado, and a misguided belief that life can be joyful by living a false life copying other peoples' lifestyle. With these words, I invite you, the reader, into this new life of realization in which the liquid love of God will usher you into that vast plain of truthful and wholesome living that is filled with nothing but love, trust, and hope.

December 2017

CHAPTER 1

To Thine Self, Be True

Above all, love each other deeply, because love covers over a multitude of sins.
                                        —1 Peter 4:8 (NIV)

Before I can love another person, I have to love myself. I have to love myself, and it is difficult to receive love when you do not love yourself. Many of us suffer from feelings of self-annihilation. Simply put, this means you have feelings of inadequacy and believe that you have to be perfect to be loved. Because of this, you aspire to become character perfect, in the hope that this will bring you love, and that you can be loved.

The truth that you must come to terms with is that you will never be perfect, for perfection belongs only to God, your Creator. However, despite your inability to achieve perfection, you can still be loved. Unfortunately, you have allowed people's expectations of you to set the standard for the level at which you believe you can and should be loved. In other words, whenever you are not approved by man, you develop feelings of rejection and low self-esteem. In turn, these feelings of rejection and self-esteem dictate to you that you are not worthy of being loved. When you adopt this self-deprecating attitude, your mind becomes conditioned to believe that you are not worthy of love that is true and deep.

One fact you must become familiar with is that people will always try to put you in a box and heap their limitations on you, almost as if they are heaping garbage on you. Worse, they will do all in their power to keep you down in that box. However, the choice of whether or not to remain in the box is yours to make. The thing to tell yourself is simply that just because people around you are mediocre does not mean you have to be mediocre. The very next thing to do is rise out of the garbage heap by shaking yourself free of these limitations. So how do you do that? You might predictably ask. The first thing you have to do is forgive yourself and forgive others. Yes, the first item on your agenda of self-liberation is self-forgiveness and the forgiveness of others.

There is a famous scientific experiment in which researchers placed a number of fleas in a container and covered it with a lid. As one would expect, the fleas kept trying to get out, and of course, all they succeeded in doing was continually hitting the lid. Finally, the researchers took off the lid, but to their surprise, the fleas abandoned all attempt to liberate themselves and fly out. What happened? You might ask. They had become conditioned to their state of incarceration. They had become conditioned to live contained. Do not be like these unfortunate fleas. Refuse to live contained. Forgive yourself for any and every thing you've done that was not right, and simply let it go. Forgive those who hurt you and just let it go. Get rid of those feelings and thoughts that hold you from loving others and loving yourself freely.

Forgiveness is the key to your kingdom of inner peace. One of the most difficult things for you to do is freely forgive someone who has offended you. This is not surprising. From childhood, you have been conditioned to believe that "an eye should go for an eye," and "a tooth should go for a tooth." That is why, for you, it is so easy to assume that holding a grudge is a perfectly normal human feeling. But to find true peace, the greatest favor you can do for yourself is to understand that holding a grudge in your heart will not make things any better. Rather, holding a grudge actually eats at your soul the way cancer eats at the cells of the body. Holding a grudge is essentially nothing but futile resentment. You owe yourself a simple yet totally healing favor. Do yourself this favor. Free yourself from the emotional burden of grievance by offering total and unconditional forgiveness. Forgive yourself. Forgive anyone who has ever offended you. Do your emotional health a favor. Do your peace of mind a favor. Do your spirituality a favor. Assist your heart to serve you better by freeing it of the load of bitterness. Nurture a true relationship with yourself by freeing your soul of silent anger. The key to your kingdom of inner peace is in your possession. The key has always resided in your heart. It is your responsibility to use it to open the doorway to your inner peace. You have the power of choice to use it or to let it go to rust.

What is that key? You may ask. It is the key of forgiveness—absolute, total, uncompromising, and unconditional forgiveness. Ultimately, it does sound like forgiveness is simple, doesn't it? Actually, it is! Simply decide today to forgive. When negative thoughts come to you, as they invariably will, deliberately change your thought to something more productive and pleasant. Speak these words to yourself: "I am forgiven. I have forgiven her. I have forgiven him," and then get on with your life. Soon, those negative thought patterns will be broken, and you will be free of those feelings.

God created you to rise higher, to break barriers, and to be free to love unconditionally. You cannot love from a pure heart when you don't love yourself. Love, as a concept, is probably the most abused, totally misunderstood, and casually thought about one in our world today. Love, to put it simply, is a sacrificial exercise. If love is not willing to be sacrificial, then it becomes pretty certain that love hasn't been tapped into yet. Yes, there is a price to love, and that price must be paid. Love is the greatest thing on earth, and like anything of immense value, it must have a price tag.

The walk of love is simply not an easy journey, and neither can it come without tremendous personal sacrifice. Each time we choose to unconditionally love another, it will cost something. It will cost time. It will cost effort. For nothing that is truly noble comes without some sacrifice. And that is why we are told to count the cost before making the commitment. Developing the walk of love is like digging for gold. To gain access to gold, you must mine for it. You must scrape through endless layers of earthy crust to gain access to the emeralds and the rubies of the earth. In the same way, true unconditional love is rarely found on the surface of life, and you must eagerly pursue and seek it in the depths of your soul.

In the thirteenth chapter of Paul's First Letter to the Corinthians and in verses 4 through 7 (NIV), he wrote, "Love is patient, love is kind. It does not envy, it does not boast, it is not proud. It does not dishonor others, it is not self-seeking, it is not easily angered, it keeps no record of wrongs. Love does not delight in evil but rejoices with the truth. It always protects, always trusts, always hopes, always perseveres." Admittedly, the scripture in 1 Corinthians chapter 13 (NIV) is a rather tough pill to swallow. However, it is the road map that God has put in place to help us in our quest to love ourselves even as we love others. Yes, it is a tough pill to swallow, but certainly one that is of immense good to your bones and marrow. Love nurtures and promotes a healthy heart. Love increases your probability of living a long and satisfactory life. You see, love doesn't keep records of wrong. It is impossible to love yourself when you refuse to let yourself become free of the hurt and wrongs that you have suffered in life. Your heart must be cleansed from corner to corner and from depth to depth while any and all memories that negatively affect your progress and ability to freely love again must be totally erased. You cease to exist when you become reluctant to love. Your very essence and your primary calling to this world are based on the singular fact that you have some loving to do, especially in today's world where all we seem to see and hear most of the time are evil deeds. Of paramount importance is that verse on which hinges our attitude, decisions, and relationships. It makes or breaks us every time. The verse is the one that says, "Love keeps no record of wrongs."

The very people Jesus died for were some of the ones who persecuted and crucified Him. But what did He say on the cross? "Father, forgive them for they know not what they do." That is how Jesus is also saying to you today, "Forgive them. Let it go. Walk away. Turn away. Love them in spite of everything. Love beyond measure. Don't hold their evil deeds toward you against them." For the Bible says that "whoever you yield your members to is your father, and you will do what your father tells you to do." Sometimes they don't even know what they are doing.

A tragic fact of holding back on love is that quite often, our prayers are held up, or we find ourselves stuck in the same place for years, just because we haven't forgiven someone. We still keep the "files" on them. We keep very precise and accurate records of the wrongs they have done to us. But until you let it all go, you are in a prison, and so you will remain incapable of loving yourself or others freely. But how many times must I forgive them, Lord? You know how Jesus answered that question in Matthew chapter 21 and verse 22 (NIV): "I tell you, not seven times, but seventy-seven times." Indeed, you must forgive them however many times they need forgiveness.

Unforgiveness is cancerous. It stops growth. It hinders even our healthy relationships with those who have done us no wrong. It hinders prayers and puts up a wall between man and God. It saps you of your joy and strength. It robs you of your vision and your hope. Get rid of it! Throw away those file cabinets. Get rid of those records of wrongs. Burn them! Rid your heart of those bad memories if you cannot learn from them. But please remember that there is always something to be learned from your experiences. Please do not misunderstand me. Love is also tough. In fact, it is unconditional, resistant, and persistent, for in actuality there is nothing wasted in our lives. Every experience has a lesson to be learned or shared. Another reality is that love does not change with the wind and the season. Love loves even when no one else is loving. Love loves even when the stakes are high. Love loves in the face of adversity. Love loves when it is lonely and broken or even broke! Love loves in action, and not only or just through words.

How does God love us? He loves us by giving, by serving, and by sacrificing. In this we can learn something important about the nature of true love or agape love. People tend to confuse eros love with agape love. Eros love is the physical and sensual love between a husband and his wife. Although this Greek term, Eros, does not appear in the Bible, eros, or erotic love, is eloquently portrayed in the Old Testament book, the Song of Solomon. God is very clear in His word about sex outside of marriage. It is forbidden. God created human beings in male and female forms and established the institution of marriage in the garden of Eden. Within marriage, sex is used for emotional and spiritual bonding and for reproduction. Some people love others only because of what those people do for them or how they make them feel. But God shows us that true love has nothing to do with what you can do for me, but everything to do with what I can do for you. The really good news about God's love is that it is not selective. Its availability is not only to those who were born with the right color of skin or on the correct continent or on the right side of the tracks or on Hollywood Boulevard, nor is it difficult to obtain. It is not reserved for only the intellectual elite or the power brokers or financial wizards. No. The enduring love of God is accessible to "whoever believes in" Jesus, the only Son of God.

God has come down to our level. This, however, is not in the sense that He has lowered His holiness or biblical standards or principles for man. His coming down to our level is only in the sense that He has made His love accessible to the average and ordinary person like me and like you. He is not a distant God who loves us only from some mystical, faraway place that is completely removed from us. No. He is not a God that can't be touched by the feelings of our infirmities. Rather, having entered into our world, He now longs to enter into our life to be an active participant in it. So God's love is clearly not based on our spiritual condition nor is it based on our moral predisposition. It isn't based on our behavior or our attitude toward him. Rather, what we can see here is that God's love for mankind is universal and unconditional. He loves everyone. This is one of the things that set Him apart from every other god held up as deity by every other world religion.

Buddhists, for example, follow an eight-fold path to enlightenment. It is not a free ride. Hindus believe in karma, meaning that your actions continually affect the way the world will treat you, that there is nothing that comes to you not set in motion by your actions. As you well know, the Bible says there are some things you reap that you did not sow. That is called God's grace. Conversely, there are some things you sowed but didn't reap. That is called God's mercy. God's love is not merely some abstract concept. It isn't just a philosophy or a theological construct. God's love was made manifest in this world through the person of Jesus Christ, the only Son of the Father. Jesus Christ came into this world in human form to reveal the love of God to us. Jesus Christ is the image of the invisible God.

Christian author, Max Lucado, writes:

> There are many reasons God saves you: to bring glory to himself, to appease his justice, to demonstrate his sovereignty. But one of the sweetest reasons God saved you is because he is fond of you. He likes having you around. He thinks you are the best thing to come down the pike in quite a while. If God had a refrigerator, your picture would be on it. If he had a wallet, your photo would be in it. He sends you flowers every spring and a sunrise every morning. Whenever you want to talk, he'll listen. He can live anywhere in the universe, and he chose your heart. And the Christmas gift he sent you in Bethlehem? Face it, my sister, my brother, GOD is crazy about you!

God loves you, and He wants you to have that deep joy and freedom with which to live out your God-given dreams. God so loves you still. The same love with which He went to the cross for you is the same love He still holds for you right now. It is beyond measure. There can't be a value added to God's love for us. There is no quantitative measure or number that quantifies His love for us. God's love is of the highest quality, being God's very best. In that, He gave us Jesus, and Jesus at His very best, which is His life. There is no qualitative formula or qualitative measure that can be assigned to His love, or which you can use to figure out His love. He just loves you. There is nothing you have possibly done wrong that can stop God from loving you. If you have sinned, ask for forgiveness and receive God's love. The Bible also says that even when we were yet sinners, God commended His love toward us. What does that say about God's love? It says God's love is unconditional. Nothing can separate you from the love of God. God so much loves you and me that He gave

His very best for you and for me. That is love. Unconditional and free!

As the scripture in John chapter 3 and verse 16 (NIV) declares: "For God so loved us that He gave His only begotten son, that whosoever shall believe in Him shall not perish but have everlasting life." The work was finished at Calvary. You have every right to abundant life, and God wants to give it to you. He loves you, and He is ready to take you to the next level in His love. Receive your abundant life today. Praise Him. To Him be all the glory. Amen.

CHAPTER 2

The Healthy Heart of Love

Blessed are the pure in heart, for they will see God.
—Matthew 5:8 (NIV)

In the month of October 2017, our church was celebrating the eighty-third year of its existence, and every Tuesday night in the month was devoted to the celebrations. I had purposefully resolved to attend each Tuesday night service. On this particular night, however, my husband had asked me to assist him with his scheduled photoshoot and asked me to remain back at home with him. But then, as it later happened, the photoshoot was canceled, and so I decided I might as well still attend the church service, and my husband joined me.

The sermon that night was truly great. Pastor Cory preached from the scripture in Habakkuk chapter 3 and verses 17 and 18 (NIV), "Though the fig tree does not bud and there are no grapes on the vines, though the olive crop fails and the fields produce no food, though there are no sheep in the pen and no cattle in the stalls, yet I will rejoice in the Lord, I will be joyful in God my Savior." The interpretation of the pastor's sermon was clear and simple. Things may not be working out as you planned them, but you can still give God all the glory and be filled with gladness that things are turning out the way He planned them. Your life may be totally upside down, with nothing but chaos all around you, but you can still shout "Hallelujah" all the same. You may be broke, bruised, and busted, but sing His praises anyway.

On our way home after the service, the route I had initially decided to take was the Atlantic City Expressway, but finding the rush-hour traffic unbearable, I chose to take Black Horse Pike instead. Sometime along the trip back home, we arrived at an intersection. I saw the light ahead of me change to yellow, so I stopped, and a second later it turned red. The next thing was that our ears were assailed by a loud screeching sound that seemed to go on for some thirty seconds, and with that came the sight of a car hurtling down the road toward us. As the car continued its relentless progress in our direction, getting closer, and ever so closer, I waited with bated breath for it to stop. Although, at some point, I thought it had stopped, but I was wrong. It didn't stop. We were in my brand-new car, a 2017 BMW X1. For me, it represented a dream come true. The car was a gleaming black-and-silver trim affair. With its beautiful interior and ambient lighting, and inspiring music playing on the radio, my 2017 BMW X1, a unique presentation planned for me by my heavenly father, was one of the personal possessions I treasured. It was just the right size. It was just the right color. It was just the right class. It came with just the right monthly payment plan. It was just right for me. It was the perfect fit.

Let me, right from the outset, make something clear. I like the nice things of this world, and I enjoy them when I have them. But the nice things of this world do not and cannot have me. At the point in time that God chose to bless me with this car, I knew it was a very special item of material blessing. I knew it was His own way of telling me, "Hey, I got you!" It was His way of saying, "I love you unconditionally." For me, this car was one prized possession that I did not have to share with anyone else. I honestly felt I could set my own boundaries, and if anyone wasn't comfortable with it, they could as well drive their own car, catch a bus, or simply walk! In my car, my word was law. You did what I said. The same policy does not play out in our home. Our home was just that: our home. It's a beautiful home. But it is 'our' home-and everything does not and will not always go the way I want it to in our home. What is most beautiful about our home is that people share and respect one another's boundaries yet are able to express themselves in their own singularly creative ways. So this car was definitely something I felt I could have exclusively for myself, a personal possession over which I had a control that I was not compelled to share with anyone. But now, what was happening?

The screeching car bore down relentlessly toward my beautiful car. It came crashing into the back of my beautiful car. The car ended its journey of destruction at the rear end of my beautiful car. It was not a love tap. It was a rather mean slap!

I was totally shaken up. My entire body was trembling. My chest was on fire while my head and lower back hurt like never before. My poor husband! Even before this, he suffered from a bad back and was a neck pain patient. The fellow that hit us certainly looked harmless enough, and at some barely lucid point, I even heard him ask how was I doing. As the EMT workers wheeled me into the ambulance, I overheard him telling my husband that he had a Dollar-a-Day insurance, meaning his insurance company would only cover about $200. My head hurt a little more. My poor BMW X1!

It was with extreme reluctance that I went to the hospital with my husband for the usual routine check after an accident. They took an EKG and many different X-rays, several of which were of my chest. When the doctor returned with the results of the tests, he told me quite a few things that I understood. But then, he added, "You have an enlarged heart." The first thought that immediately occurred to me was about *The Good Doctor*, a new show that showcases autism in all aspects and the beauty that can open up to you if you would just open your mind to knowledge and comprehension. The good doctor obviously did not want to deliberately lie to his patients, but it might seem that there is this subterranean agreement in the medical field that it is better to either outrightly lie to a patient, avoid the truth entirely, or ingeniously deflect to another aspect of the situation so as not to precipitate fear and hopelessness. Well, Dr. Good, in his autistic wisdom, appears convinced that to tell the patient the truth is not only their right, but that it is also the right and ethical thing to do. So I found myself asking myself: "Did he just say I have an enlarged heart and that I will need to follow up with my doctor, preferably my cardiologist, if I have one?" Eventually, I was discharged and went back home with many medical papers. It was when I got home and read over my discharge papers that I ran into the term ischemic myocardial for the first time in my life.

What in the world is ischemic myocardial? I immediately went into research mode. Apparently, ischemic myocardial, otherwise known as myocardial ischemia, occurs when blood flow to the heart muscle is reduced, preventing it from receiving sufficient oxygen. The low blood flow decreases the amount of oxygen the heart muscle receives. The reduced blood flow is usually the result of a partial or complete blockage of the heart's arteries, which are called coronary arteries. Myocardial ischemia can damage the heart muscle, reducing its ability to pump efficiently. Eventually, in its effort to pump suf-ficient blood to meet the demands of the rest of the body, the heart muscle becomes tired and flabby, resulting in a general enlargement of the heart. I also learned that a sudden severe blockage of a coro-nary artery is what sometimes leads to a heart attack, otherwise called a "coronary."

The long and short of it all was that I now had an enlarged heart, or so I had been led to believe. An enlarged heart can give serious cause for concern. Why didn't my wonderful doctor inform me about the urgency of seeing a cardiologist? Why didn't my good doctor educate me on what ischemic myocardial actually is, what it does, and the adverse effects it can have on the heart? Let me tell you that this had turned out a really crazy day. Quite a few supernatural things were happening that just didn't seem right, resulting in me getting the short end of the stick in that day.

Now, let me explain why the day had turned out so dysfunc-tional for me. The first thing was that I had argued with my husband regarding my driving record versus his driving record. The second thing was that as I went to pick up a script from my primary doctor earlier that afternoon, and as I was going into the doctor's office, these words just came tumbling out of my mouth: "Healthy heart, healthy attitude. Healthy attitude, healthy heart. Sick heart. Sick heart." I said to the Lord, "My heart isn't that healthy." Thirdly, at 1:00 p.m., as my husband went into his doctor's office to obtain some information, one of the workers, a young lady, was on her way out to lunch, but she took the time and trouble to assist us. A remarkable coincidence concerning this particular lady was to unfold much later in the day. I recall that on our way home from church, before the accident occurred, I was talking about this young lady to my husband. Incredibly, when we arrived to the hospital at 10:00 p.m. after the accident, the same lady turned out to be our admitting nurse at the hospital!

I draw certain spiritual inferences from all that occurred on that day. Without doubt, God was using the accident to test my faith. Yes, a material possession, my beautiful BMW X1, that I placed so much value on, had been terribly damaged. Back to the scripture in Habakkuk chapter 3 and verses 17 and 18 (NIV): "Though the fig tree does not bud and there are no grapes on the vines, though the olive crop fails and the fields produce no food, though there are no sheep in the pen and no cattle in the stalls, yet I will rejoice in the Lord, I will be joyful in God my Savior." Indeed, things may not have turned out as I would have wished, but my mouth can still be filled with words and songs of praise. My gorgeous car may be damaged, but I can still revel in God's unconditional love for sparing my life and that of my husband.

The second spiritual lesson I may have learned came as a result of my visit to my primary doctor a few days later. Amazingly, he told me that I did not have an enlarged heart! He went further to tell me that the measurements of my heart size are definitely within the normal range for me. I couldn't help thinking to myself, "What is this all about? Why was I subjected to the initial trepidation that I had an enlarged heart, when, at the end of it all, it was all a false alarm after all?" The answer did not take long in coming. God had used the entire frightening episode, from the accident itself to the false yet alarming diagnosis of ischemic myocardial, to give me an understanding of the relationship between the spiritual heart and the physical heart. A healthy spiritual heart, which is the healthy heart that reflects the unconditional love of God, and which insists on praising Him in all circumstances, seemingly good or seemingly bad, is what makes for a healthy physical heart. Conversely, a sick spiritual heart, one that lacks love, cannot see the need to appreciate the mighty wonders of God in life's experiences and therefore cannot continually praise Him. It is this sick spiritual heart that makes for an equally sick physical heart.

In conclusion, another understanding that we may arrive at is that the practice of the true components of unconditional love, which are kindness, compassion, and forgiveness, may also be related to the emotional anatomy of the heart. You see, the emotional anatomy of the heart seems to be very much like the botanical anatomy of the onion. To arrive at the layer of lack of love, both for self and for others, and peel it off, we must first, and in succession, peel off the layers of anger, sadness, fear, and hurt. There is a reality that your physical health can be adversely effected by *your spiritual condition.*

Yes, the healthy heart of love is a loving and forgiving heart, and the very compassion that it proclaims is in the same instance clear enough indication that you are ready to be a willing receiver of the unconditioned and liquid love of God. Hallelujah!

CHAPTER 3

The Yoke of Offense

Do not pay attention to every word people say, or you may hear your servant cursing you.
—Ecclesiastes 7:21 (NIV)

It is amazing how, for many years, a word can remain basically of no particular significance to us, and then one day, it suddenly becomes quite important. The word *offense* is one such word. An offense, being something that constitutes a violation of what is considered to be right, is a word that takes on some importance between two people and for different reasons. This is because one person gives the offense while the other person is the victim of the offense.

Each day, we come across people who have stories and accusations of offenses that they have suffered at the hand of another person. Yes, offense has become a reproach to the special grace that is the unconditional love of God. Many an offense is done to another in secret. Many an offense is done in a clandestine manner. It reminds me of how a lot of Americans consumed illicit liquor in their homes, and in speakeasies, during the Prohibition era of the Great Depression of the 1930s. The funny thing was that patrons of such illicit drinking clubs thought the authorities did not know of the existence of such underground clubs. They were wrong. The government, more often than not, knew about them. The government was not mocked. Judgment was still on its way for the violators of the law.

God, also, cannot be mocked. You see, the Word tells us very clearly that what is done in the dark will surely come to light. That is why the scripture in Galatians chapter 6 and verse 7 (NIV) also declares, "Do not be deceived; God cannot be mocked. A man reaps what he sows." Although the judgment of God has not come yet, many have already fallen into their own personal judgment.

The law of cause and effect is very precise. Indeed, the outcome of our deeds is merely an expression of the law of cause and effect because there is a celestial order, which is simply God's own perfect order, to all our affairs. This order is never in error, and simply because there may be a long interval between an action and its result, most people have the unfortunate tendency to forget the cause and rather concern themselves with the effect. The day of reckoning is still on its way. In fact, could the coronavirus pandemic be a prelude to the day of reckoning for America? God is not an evil God and cannot be tempted with evil. He has not made us robots but has given us free will to choose different paths to take in life. Could our decisions be what has brought us to this crisis in America? Yes, a man will always reap what he sows.

Offenses are like army ants. Army ants are restless and ravenous. Army ant colonies are nature's Mongol hordes. They kill and eat anything in their way, digesting it even as they tear it apart! They are always on the move and ravage anything and everyone in their path. When an army ant colony is on the move, anything that stands in their way is totally overwhelmed. They waste no time in eating and then digesting because as they are dicing up their prey with their strong mandibles, they spread a dissolving acid, and as soon as flesh becomes liquidized, they simply eat it and keep going. Offenses are like these army ants. They have come home to roost. Offenses are ferocious and merciless in their onslaught. They dissolve all ounces of faith that we have in others. The judgment on a lot of people is coming to roost because of the many bad seeds sown in the lives of God's precious people. Offenses are very much like army ants because they come to attach themselves to you and to entangle you with the yoke of bondage and to ultimately consume you, very much in the same manner that the very ferocious and aggressive army ant fastens its prey with its powerful jaws to dice it into pieces, entangle it with its acidic secretion to liquefy it, and then consume it.

According to Apostolic Minister Ryan Johnson, in a very prophetic ministration in 2017,

> When offenses take root, the first place it's com-
> ing after is your mind. If offense can attach itself
> to your thoughts, it owns your ability to process
> understanding. The moment offense attaches
> itself to your mind, the ability to have clarity and
> peace is diminished, as everything now becomes
> about feeding every thought that is only directed
> at the hurt through offense.

Yet you need clarity and peace of mind to be able to worship
God in truth and without distraction. Offense allows the flesh to
disallow the spirit from gaining access to the issues of God. This is
eloquently illustrated by the scripture in Romans chapter 8, verses 5
through 8 (NIV),

> For those who live according to the flesh set their
> minds on the things of the flesh, but those who
> live according to the Spirit, the things of the
> Spirit. To be carnally minded is death, but to be
> spiritually minded is life and peace, for the carnal
> mind is hostile toward God, for it is not subject
> to the law of God, nor indeed can it be, and those
> who are in the flesh cannot please God.

This concept works the same way in relation to an open wound.
That is, in much the same way that offense grieves the spirit, that is
also how a germ assaults an open wound. If you had a surgery or say
you sustained a cut for any reason and you contracted a germ, it will
travel straight to the open wound and infect it. This is one reason
why hospitals do not sanction long stays of recovery in the hospital.
A long stay in the hospital increases the chance of contracting a new
germ, in what is called a nosocomial infection, and, naturally, this
could result in a serious setback for the patient.

Offenses are so powerful that they affect your thoughts in such a way as to actually alter your perspective. Picture the following scenario in your mind, if you will. A man is traveling south on a highway. An approaching car traveling in the opposite direction slows down a little. The other driver rolls down his window and yells at the man traveling south, shouting "Pig" at him. The southern traveler responds out of his own window, "Back at you!" A few minutes later, he crashes into a pig crossing the highway! The man was not calling the southern driver a pig, he was trying to warn him that a pig was just up ahead and to be careful. This is so often how other people hurl their "garbage of words" at us. Everyone seems to be attacking us. Every word that comes to our ear gate is perceived as criticism or negatively motivated. In other words, to our own detriment, we choose to construe every word spoken to us in negative terms. It can get so bad that it begins to affect your spiritual hearing, and you begin to separate yourself from the love of God. Put differently, if you do not deliberately start to separate yourself from perceived offense, you soon start to separate yourself from the love of God.

The scripture in Romans chapter 8, verse 35 (NIV) states, "Who shall separate us from the love of Christ? Shall trouble or hardship or persecution or famine or nakedness or danger or sword?" Offense can easily separate us from the love of God. A person who is victimized by offense is unable to see or hear the issues of God correctly, and if those offenses are not addressed, they will eventually nurture in that person a negative mind-set and damage his most intimate relationships.

Indeed, if we allow ourselves to become victimized by offense, we will be unable to perceive God, His love, and His counsel in correct context. This brings me to the question of perception. However, to deal properly with perception, at least in the context of offense, we must also consider another word; that word is deception. But what is the difference between perception and deception? Perception, being the ability to be aware of something through the senses, is what exists in the mind as a representation of what is seen or heard, or as a formulation, as in a plan, for instance. Deception, on the other hand, is to trick or mislead someone. It also means to lead someone astray or to frustrate them by underhanded deeds. So deception, as an act, is initiated from without, being an external influence which acts on the inside. There is an interrelatedness between perception and deception. This is it. Our perceptions can cause us to be vulnerable to deception. A man's perception is the sum total of all he believes himself to be. The verse in Proverbs that says that it is as a man thinks in his heart that he is actually means that it is what a man believes about himself that he becomes in his reality. Indeed, whatever a man can conceive in his mind, he can achieve. It is a man's attitude that will determine his altitude in life.

Generally, it is the wrong type of perception that causes a breakdown in relationships, fragmentation in the body of Christ, and alienation from our goals and dreams. Our perceptions, when not properly framed, can work against the very things we desire for a life of joy, and these are unity and harmony. When our perceptions are off focus, they can sometimes become colored by our selfishness, wrong motives, and hidden agendas, and rather than seeing as God sees, we begin to see through a very dark and alien prism. The scripture in Ephesians chapter 4, verse 3 (NIV) says, "Make every effort to keep the unity of the Spirit through the bond of peace." It is this kind of perception, one of self-centeredness, and one that is based on the "it's all about me" syndrome that is the cause of divorce and wrecking our homes. Just like it happened with Eve, it is hard to deprive yourself of transient pleasure when your thoughts are always on what will make you, and only you, happy. Our eyes are wide open, but we are not really seeing. For it is only when we start seeing through the eyes of introspection that we really begin to see. But, for now, much of our lens are covered with filters of envy; jealousy, lust, greed, hypocrisy, covertness, strife, and slander.

Finally, I asked the Lord to give me insight into how Eve's perception caused her to become vulnerable to deception. This is what the Lord told me. The enemy, the devil, employs two prototypes of tools to deceive us. He has one type for females and another type for males. In the scripture in Genesis chapter 3, verse 1 (NIV), we read about how the devil insinuated himself into Eve's perception through deception: "Now the serpent was more crafty than any of the wild animals the Lord God had made. He said to the woman, 'Did God really say, "You must not eat from any tree in the garden?"'" So from this scripture, we can see that the enemy's tool of deception in the woman is to create an element of doubt and confusion in her. Did God really say, or did He actually say? These become the questions in a woman's mind, and she becomes confused, and doubt creeps into her mind. When a woman gets a word from the Lord, the enemy comes immediately to visit her, bringing his own false word to counteract the word of the Lord. Most females are indecisive. They just can't seem to make up their minds easily, at least, it is seemingly so. Maybe females just like to explore all possible options before taking a decision, leaving themselves open to the subtle suggestions of the enemy. After a while, they can't differentiate between God's picture and the devil's picture. In the final analysis, did God really say what He said? Yes, He did!

In stark contrast, Adam did not even give the proposition of eating the apple the slightest thought. He simply delved into it! He just ate. We can see that, for men, the enemy uses a different tool. The enemy lulls a man into the false belief that he has power whereas he does not possess any power, especially in areas where he has not submitted himself totally to God. This, truly, is extremely dangerous territory for men, but they do not know it.

That feeling of self-assurance in the face of the devil's exploits has brought many a man down. The pathetic story of Samson's fall in the hands of Delilah is an eloquent example of this. Samson, a man of legendary strength and a Nazirite, was in love with Delilah. Delilah was bribed by the Philistines to discover the source of Samson's strength. After three failed attempts at doing so, she finally goads Samson into revealing that his incomparable strength is derived from his hair. While he slept, Delilah orders a servant to cut Samson's hair, enabling her to turn him over to the Philistines. He fell. And that is how so many men are falling on daily basis because they are dependent on a power that they do not really possess, and they don't possess this power because they have not totally submitted to the will of God in being deceitful, unfaithful, dishonest, and unreliable in the divine assignment God has given them to honor and to love their partners.

Offense is very powerful indeed. But you are the only one who can confer this power on offense. The reason why offense is so powerful is that it affects your thoughts negatively. The truth is that your thoughts are the container of your actions. This is how it works out. First you think it, then that thought travels to your heart, and then you feel it, and finally, behavior that is consistent with that thought follows. Thoughts are very powerful entities, and not only are they powerful, but they can also be life changing. What is even more significant, they can end up defining you, what you believe, and what you stand for. This means that, ultimately, your thoughts can actually determine your direction in life. As the scripture in Proverbs chapter 23, verse 7 (NIV) says, "For as a man thinks in his heart, so he is." Your thoughts can make you, and your thoughts can break you. That is why mindfulness about the things of God is so important. The more you insist on occupying your mind space with thoughts of the love of God, the more you disallow offense from creating thoughts that will detract you from your destiny. That is why the scripture in Proverbs chapter 4, verse 23 (NIV) emphatically says, "Above all else, guard your heart, for everything you do flows from it."

In conclusion, the final outcome of your love walk with God, and by extension, the quality of your life, will be determined by the quality of your thoughts with regard to offense. Your destiny is too important for you to toy with offenses. These words by Ralph Waldo Emerson, the great American philosopher, puts it all in correct perspective: "Sow a thought and you reap an action; sow an act and you reap a habit; sow a habit and you reap a character; sow a character and you reap a destiny."

I leave you with the words of Paul, in his letter to the Philippians, in chapter 4, verse 8 (NIV): "Finally, brothers and sisters, whatever is true, whatever is noble, whatever is right, whatever is pure, whatever is lovely, whatever is admirable; if anything is excellent or praiseworthy; think about such things."

CHAPTER 4

That Place of Pain

*"For I know the plans I have for you," declares the
LORD, "plans to prosper you and not to harm you,
plans to give you hope and a future."*
—Jeremiah 29:11 (NIV)

Along my road to the place of God's unconditional love, I found
myself asking one question: "Why do you keep bringing me back
here?" Because it seems as if this is a place where you can get stuck.
Does this resonate with you? Do you feel like you are going around
and around over the same territory? Do you feel like you are stuck in
some particular spot? The sinking feeling in your heart is that your
life appears to be moving, yet you appear to remain stationary, very
much as if you found yourself on a conveyor belt that is moving
relentlessly while you appear to be its immobile passenger. You can't
seem to make good progress, and you feel like your life is wasting
away. The result of this is that you feel that you have relinquished
control to something or someone out of yourself that is now guiding
your life. It is a sensation of total lack of control, and it is not a very
safe or comfortable feeling. You want your life back.

You are truly baffled. Why would God want you to go back to,
or even make you go back, to the place you so desperately want to
move away from? What could possibly be in that place where you
got stuck, and whatever it is, is it of such great value that you have to
remain there for any appreciable length of time? It is also at this point
that you realize that you seem to have arrived at a fork in the road.

And it is at this fork in the road that you suddenly discover what you must possess before you can make further progress by choosing which path to follow. Yes, you now know what is at that place. It is your freedom. Your freedom is in that place—that fork in the road. Your crucial decision now is whether to move forward and live your life to the fullest or take a path that leads nowhere. You will have to take one of the two options.

Almost invariably, that place where you get stuck is the place of forgiveness. That is why your very freedom itself is what you need to reclaim before you can move on. And this is because it is in practicing total and unconditional forgiveness that you can obtain this freedom and make progress. Yes, forgiveness. That little deadly word. That word, whose inability to practice can kill every life-giving blessing in your life.

We have already talked about forgiveness in some depth in chapter 1 of this book, in which we spoke of the potency of a life lived in a state of forgiveness and the despair of a life lived in a state of unforgiveness. An inability to freely forgive saps you of your joy. It saps you of your energy. It saps you of your ability to create and in the process, be a blessing to others by making a difference in your world and in the world at large. Should you insist on moving along without forgiveness, you will find that it has consumed you, and your future will offer nothing but a life filled with pain and disappointment. That is why that place where you appear to be stuck is actually a place of pain. It is because it is a place of unforgiveness. It is when you shed the burden of unforgiveness that you release yourself from the pain, and you can then take the path that leads to a life of joy and fulfill-ment. If you don't shed this burden at this fork in the road, every-thing you attempt to do, and every relationship you find yourself in, and in which you would desire to thrive, will be paralyzed in some way or the other because you are still holding on to the ugly past. And to assuage our pain, we invariably need to heap the blame on someone. Most of us find it easier to simply blame God for all that deep hurt and disappointment. Well, in real terms, we may be right. Yes, He knows about all that hurt and disappointment. But actu-ally, He is neither wasting our time nor is He wasting His. He has a purpose. He always has a purpose. God's ultimate purpose is to use that hurt and disappointment to bring you into a wealthy place. As a being of flesh, your argument may be, "But I would rather have my daughter back or my husband or my business or my legs or my sight or ministry or my mother." But the reality is simply this: you cannot bring back what is gone from this world. You cannot bring back what has gone from your world. You are left with the only viable option. You have to take one path. And that is the path of trust. You have to trust in God's love. He is always at work on us, and this is because He loves us anyway. That is why the scripture in Matthew chapter 11, verse 28 (NIV) says, "Come to me, all you who are weary and burdened, and I will give you rest." That is why God's purpose for all your pain, hurt, and disappointment is to take you to that wealthy place of rest. That is why you must put your trust and rest your mind on Him totally so as to validate the prophet's words in Isaiah chapter 26, verse 3 (NIV): "You will keep in perfect peace those whose minds are steadfast, because they trust in you."

No one in our world is immune to evil. Evil is simply a part of life. Don't forget that Lucifer himself was one of God's fallen angels. So Satan has been a part of the world from the beginning of time. After all, when Job was going to be subjected to His devastating trials, was it not to God that Satan turned to obtain permission to inflict pain on the poor man? This means that God has always had His purpose for allowing pain to be visited upon us. You want the promise of a pain free life. Well, I have news for you. There is no life that is pain-free. Ours is a freewill universe, in which God gives us the power of choice to either follow Him or not follow Him. If we refuse to follow Him, we leave ourselves exposed to the devices of Satan, and evil can easily find a way into our life. Is it any wonder that you are drowning in great sorrow? God can, however, stem the flow of your tears. It is time to reach out to God to take control. It is time to let go and enjoy the life you have left. The only way you can make the most of that time is to stop going over the same territory or visiting the same hurt or previous bad experiences. It is time to stop second-guessing yourself. Continually asking yourself "why" is a mere exercise in futility. You can only speculate about the "why." You cannot come into a full comprehension of

God's motives just yet. You will only understand God's intention when you come face-to-face with Him. In the meantime, simply enjoy your journey. We are here for just a short time for our life is like a flower whose color fades away all too soon.

When all is said and done, what does it mean to be stuck? The word "stuck" immediately brings into our mind other words like fastened, attached, glued, pinned. These other words allow us to appreciate what it means to be stuck. But you need to realize that you are now on a healing trail, and you need closure of the past for that thing that hurt you so badly to relinquish its tight hold on you. You need to unglue yourself from it. You need to unfasten the seat belt of agony that is pinning you down to your seat of pain. You have allowed your situation to become so bad that everyone you know and every influence you have come under close scrutiny. But always remember that no one gets away with anything because everything bears its own consequences. God is not asking you to excuse what has happened to you, but He is asking you to trust Him because in knowing what is best, He will also do what is right.

So now, you can finally answer the question "Why do you keep bringing me back here?" You have to go back to that place of pain—that place where you were stuck—so that you can pass your test and move on to the next level in your life. You are not stuck because you can't. Rather, you are stuck because you won't. Refuse to permit rebellion to stand in the way of your freedom. Refuse to allow ignorance to hinder your ability to really enjoy your life journey.

There are so many lessons to be learned at the place where you are stuck. Nothing is wasted in your life for God promises to turn your ashes into beauty. One thing I am learning with each passing day about our Father is that He is persistent. He only wants the best for your life. Therefore, He will continue to work with you until you surrender to His divine will. After all, He has been collecting your tears for such a long time. As the psalmist declares in the scripture of chapter 56, verse 8, "You number my wanderings; You put my tears into Your bottle; Are they not in Your book?" Indeed, He said He will bottle up every tear, and your tears will become your oil of joy. Amen.

CHAPTER 5

That Place of Rest

God's promise that we may enter his place of rest still stands. We are afraid that some of you think you won't enter his place of rest.

—Hebrews 4:1 (NIV)

In our love walk with God, there are two very important places where we can find rest with Him. And it is in these two places that we can, as His children, truly justify all our efforts to lay claim to the inheritance of His kingdom. The two places are the resting place of Victory and the resting place of Faith.

To be victorious means to be triumphant in battle. It means to defy the odds and emerge the winner in a confrontation. It also means to subdue our enemies. In our privileged position as God's children, we are programmed to subdue our enemies. However, we need to know that, in our arsenal for battle, two war strategies are available to us—a defensive strategy and an offensive strategy. The first thing an army general will tell you is that it is totally impossible to win a war by fighting it with a defensive strategy. At the very best, a defensive stance should merely be a backup to a very active offensive one. To defeat Satan, we need to adopt an offensive strategy. The reason we haven't made substantial progress in our quest to defeat Satan is because we are using a defensive strategy. Our problem is that when the enemy comes, we put our hands up and try to defend ourselves. That will, and can, never work. We need aggression. We need aggression at the front line of battle.

Offensive warfare is aggressive. Being aggressive calls for each of us to develop an attitude of action—an attitude of forward movement that is bold, courageous, and audacious. Jesus put it very clearly when He said that the violent take the kingdom of heaven by force. As it says in the scripture in Matthew chapter 11, verse 12 (NIV), "And from the days of John the Baptist until now the kingdom of heaven suffereth violence, and the violent take it by force." Strong's Concordance defines the word *violent* as "to seize or take hold of forcefully." Traditionally, we have labored under the misguided preoccupation of teaching people how to protect themselves against the enemy. This is very necessary, of course, as it is foolhardy to foolishly expose oneself to the machinations of the devil without any form of protection. But the season has come for us not just to teach on how to peacefully protect ourselves against Satan's ploys, but to actively raise up an army to invade his territory. The Commander and General of our army, our Lord Jesus Christ, has already conquered the enemy and gained victory on our behalf. It is now up to us to boldly seize and take possession of the territory that He has conquered for us.

Paul states in the scripture in Ephesians chapter 6, verses 12 through 18 (NIV), that we are engaged in a warfare, and that we have weapons with which we must fight. We wrestle not against a human opponent. Rather, we are wrestling with rulers, authorities, the powers who govern this world of darkness, and spiritual forces that control evil in the heavenly world. Their primary focus is to defile, enslave, hinder, frustrate, kill, and destroy us. We must learn how to wage offensive warfare which will help us advance into Satan's territory. That is why the scripture in 2 Corinthians chapter 10, verses 4 and 5 (NIV) says, "For the weapons of our warfare are not carnal, but mighty in God for pulling down strongholds, casting down arguments and every high thing that exalts itself against the knowledge of God, bringing every thought into captivity to the obedience of Christ." The good news is that God has given us mighty weapons with which to counter satanic attacks and influences. Not only can we resist the devil's influence in our lives; we can actually employ offensive warfare to destroy his influence in the lives of others. However, in order to be effective in our warfare, we must know what these weapons are and how to use them effectively. Those offensive weapons are six in number.

The first is the Word of God, which Paul describes as the sword of the spirit in Ephesians 6:17 (NIV): "Take the helmet of salvation and the sword of the Spirit, which is the word of God." God is calling us to wield our swords against the enemy. Openly declaring His Word will serve to beat back all that opposes the manifestation of God's divine will and purpose for our lives. When Jesus was tempted three times in the wilderness by Satan, He overcame the devil using the Word of God: "It is written…" This silenced the devil, and he departed. The reason why we can speak God's Word with confidence is because God Himself declared in the scripture in Isaiah chapter 55, verse 11 (NIV) that what He says will come to pass: "So shall my word be that goes forth out of my mouth; it shall not return unto me void, but it shall accomplish that which I please and purpose, and it shall prosper in the thing for which I sent it."

The second offensive weapon is praise and worship. When we worship, we focus on God's holiness and His worthiness. When we praise Him for what He has done, we also praise Him for who He is. Praise is a bold declaration while worship is a humble bow to a holy God. The scripture in Psalm 29, verse 2 (NIV) says, "Give unto the Lord the glory due to His name; Worship the Lord in the beauty of holiness." When we worship, we receive direction and revelation. Worship releases the hand of God in our battle. Praise, on the other hand, opens the door to God's presence, and it is a weapon in spiritual warfare. God inhabits Himself in our praises. That is why the scripture in Psalm 22, verse 3 (NIV) says, "But thou art holy, O thou that inhabits the praises of Israel." In other words, God dwells in the atmosphere of His praise, and when we offer praise to God, we are acknowledging Him as our King.

The third offensive weapon is pleading the blood of Jesus, and it means to apply the blood to our lives and circumstances just like the Israelites applied the blood of a lamb to their doorposts and were protected from the destroyer. It means to stand on the spiritual rights that are legally ours through the blood that Jesus shed for the forgiveness of our sins. Yes, indeed, the blood of Jesus gives you rights over the devil and rights with God. You see, we are in a blood covenant with God, which is why the scripture in Revelations 12, verse 11 (NIV) says, "And they overcame him by the Blood of the Lamb and by the Word of their testimony and they loved not their life even unto death…" It is this covenant that provides provision for our every need, including protection from satanic attack.

The fourth offensive weapon is prayer. Prayer is a relationship in which we humbly communicate with God, knowing that He hears us. As the scripture in 1 John chapter 5, verses 14 and 15 (NIV) tells us, "This is the confidence we have in approaching God: that if we ask anything according to his will, he hears us. And if we know that he hears us; whatever we ask, we know that we have what we asked of him." God answers prayers that are in agreement with His will and responds in a way that is in our best interest. No matter how big the problem the enemy is using to attack us, when we ask God for help, He breaks that attack and rescues us.

The fifth offensive weapon is the word of our testimony. Giving our testimony on how we overcame our trials with the help of the Lord not only glorifies God, but is a powerful offensive weapon against the devil. The enemy doesn't like it when we share with others about all the things that the Lord has done on our behalf since our testimony not only increases our faith, but the faith of those who are listening to us. That is why the scripture in Revelation chapter 12, verse 11 (NIV) says, "And they overcame him by the blood of the Lamb, and by the word of their testimony."

The last weapon is the name of Jesus. Jesus said to His disciples in John chapter 14, verses 13 and 14 (NIV), "And whatever you ask in My name, that I will do, that the Father may be glorified in the Son. If you ask anything in My name, I will do it." His name represents all of His finished work on the cross. His name represents victory over the devil's entire realm. When the name of Jesus Christ is invoked, it carries all of the power and distinction God gave to it. God raised Jesus from the dead, elevated Him to His right hand, and gave Jesus a name above every name. The enemy has to yield to the almighty name of Jesus. There is nothing that can stand up to His Name. Every time the enemy hears the name of Jesus, he trembles.

Yes, indeed, our confrontations with the enemy call for offensive warfare. Notice Caleb's attitude when he returned from his spying expedition to the promised land. He did not give the enemy any latitude to come up against him. Instead, he was the first to attack offensively by saying, "Let us go up at once and possess it for we are well able to overcome it." (Numbers 13:30, NIV). His attitude was one of total and unwavering victory, for he knew His God and believed in His promises. He was willing to act with boldness. He knew that victories can only be won through offensive warfare. Only through offensive warfare, led by the Holy Spirit, can we stop holding the fort and validate the scripture in Romans chapter 8, verse 37 (NIV), "No, in all these things we are more than conquerors through him who loved us." Herein lies that place of rest called victory.

The second place of rest is that of faith. The rest of faith is a rest in service. It is also, at the same time, coupled with a yoke for activity. That means, inherent in the confidence of a rest in faith is an active and vibrant participation in one's walk of love with God. A Christian will never find rest in being idle. There is no unrest greater than that of the sluggard. As the scripture in Proverbs chapter 13, verse 4 (NIV) says, "The soul of the sluggard craves and gets nothing, But the soul of the diligent is made fat."

For you to lay any valid claim to your rest, you have to take Christ's yoke and be actively engaged in His service, in much the same manner that the bullock has the yoke put on its neck and commences to obey his master. The rest of heaven is not the rest of sleep because as the scripture in Revelation chapter 7, verse 15 (NIV) says, "They serve him day and night in his temple; and he who sits on the throne will shelter them with his presence." It is in this "sheltering us with his presence" that we find our place of rest in our faith in Him. We will always be at rest, yet in another sense, we rest not at day nor at night.

Holy activity in heaven is perfect. It is true rest to the mind of the child of God. It is rest on the wings. It is rest in motion. It is rest in service. That rest is one with the yoke on and not with the yoke off. We are required to enter into this service voluntarily. We are to take His yoke upon us voluntarily. Although the yoke sometimes has a negative connotation, we actually come to the Lord yoked to something. So when we enter into the rest of God and we are expecting to be free from the yoke of the world, we are only switching yokes, for God tells us to take His yoke upon us. That is why the scripture in Hebrews chapter 4, verse 1 (NIV) says, "Therefore, since the promise of entering His rest still stands, let us be careful that none of you be found to have fallen short of it."

Our souls are made for activity, and when we are set free through Jesus Christ, we are set free from the activities of our self-righteousness and the slavery of our sin. We must continue to do something in His vineyard, and we shall never find rest until we find something to do for the Lord. There is a line of distinction between a yoke that is an indication of working and a burden that is the emblem of enduring. It is in man's mortal nature that he must do, or endure, or else his spirit will stagnate and be very far from the rest he so fervently seeks. The scripture in Matthew chapter 11, verse 29 (NIV) says, "Take my yoke upon you and learn from me, for I am gentle and humble in heart, and you will find rest for your souls." That verse illustrates that the best place of rest is the rest of a man who is already at rest. It celebrates the repose of the soul of a man who has received an already given rest and now discovers the found rest. It is the rest of a learner.

In conclusion, no words can put it better than the scripture in Hebrews chapter 4, verses 9 through 11 (NIV): "There remains, then, a Sabbath-rest for the people of God; for anyone who enters God's rest also rests from their works, just as God did from His. Let us, therefore, make every effort to enter that rest, so that no one will perish by following their example of disobedience."

CHAPTER 6

Weapons for Restoration

Therefore, if anyone is in Christ, the new creation
has come. The old has gone, the new is here!
—2 Corinthians 5:17 (NIV)

One morning, as I sat in still repose, seeking the Lord, He spoke to me. His voice came clearly and strongly, "They're coming in on broken pieces." At that surreal moment, a vision flashed across my consciousness. In that vision, I saw some women. They were in a boat on a tranquil river. And they were rowing the boat with their bare hands. Soon, they approached the shore. That was when I saw that they were actually not in a boat but rowing in on broken pieces. What were these broken pieces? The broken pieces were broken marriages, broken health, broken finances, broken dreams and visions, and broken relationships, between daughter and daughter, between mother and daughter, and between mother and son.

I cried out in anguish. The sight was almost too much to bear. "Why, God! But why?"

I waited in silence for His response. It did not take too long in coming. He said, "I will show you three weapons. These weapons are what these women will need for the restoration of all that are broken in their lives so that they can pick up these pieces and put them back together to become whole again."

"Here I am, Lord. Show me," I replied soberly. That was when He showed me the three weapons you need for the restoration of your broken life. They are the three weapons you need to become a receiver of the liquid love of God. Here they are. Listen.

The first weapon is humility. In the scripture in Proverbs chapter 18, verse 12 (NIV), it says, "Before his downfall, a man's heart is haughty, but humility comes before honor." Indeed, humility will have to come before honor. Why is this so? The reason is really quite simple. With God, there is always a process. Let us look at the sequence. First, a man develops an exaggerated concept of his own importance before his creator. Then his downfall comes. But for him to be restored to his place of honor, he must develop humility. Humility denotes a process. That process is suffering. He must progress through the process of suffering. When he has successfully passed through that phase of suffering, he becomes humbled. It is after passing through the humiliation of suffering that humility finally comes to the man, and then he is now qualified for honor. Finally, honor brings the glory of God into his situation. That is why the scripture in Psalm chapter 48, verse 2 (NIV) states, "Beautiful for situations, the joy of the whole earth is Mount Zion."

I will illustrate what humility can achieve in the life of a person by relating the story line of the movie *Men of Honor*, a film that centered around the life of the first African American navy diver, Carl Brashear, a role played by actor Cuba Gooding Jr. The story is set at a time when white men were steeped in bigotry and racial prejudice. The mind-set of the day was that black people were stupid and lazy, and perhaps even subhuman. In 1948, Carl Brashear left his native Kentucky and his life as a sharecropper to join the United States Navy. As a crew member on the salvage ship USS *Hoist*, he was inspired by the bravery of one of the divers and determined that he would overcome racism and become the first African American Navy diver.

Given the extreme racist tendencies of that period, that was a rather tall ambition for a black man. It was a Herculean task trying to prove himself as he was given the toughest assignments called the worst names conceivable and deliberately goaded to the limits of his very wits, all so that he would give up. He never did! However, at each station Brashear reached in his naval career, he was faced with men who could decide his fate in any manner they chose. There were men who could open a door and men who could close it. But each time these men wanted to say no, they ended up saying yes instead in spite of the racism that was so deeply embedded in them.

Yes, the Lord showed me these men; men could not say no to the humility of a man. This is so reflective of the spirit of God! Why? Humility comes before honor.

Clearly, humiliation and humbling are two separate, though similar, experiences. Humiliation is a noun and is the act of reducing someone to a lower position in the eyes of other people. Humbling, on the other hand, is a derivative of the verb *humble*, which means not to be proud or arrogant, but rather, to be modest. No example presents these two experiences better than the story of Joseph in the Bible. Joseph's humiliation was serial and total. First, he was sold into slavery by his own brothers. Later, in the course of diligently attending to his duties, he was falsely accused of raping Potiphar's wife and was sent off to prison. Eventually, however, and in a most remarkable twist to the series of events, Joseph became governor of the entire province. His humility, through suffering, finally brought him honor.

So we can see that suffering actually squeezes out the pride from a person and leaves behind the sweet fragrance of the spirit of humility of God on the person. King David summarized the benefit of suffering humiliation when in Psalm 119, verse 71 (NIV), he said, "It was good for me to be afflicted so that I might learn your decrees." Brashear, Joseph, and David all went from obscurity to prominence, and from poverty to financial stability, through the process of humility.

The second powerful weapon for restoration is giving. In the scripture in Acts chapter 20, verse 35 (NIV), Paul says, "In everything I did, I showed you that by this kind of hard work we must help the weak, remembering the words the Lord Jesus himself said: 'It is more blessed to give than to receive.'" In the context of this scripture, I am not necessarily referring to money although giving monetarily makes you more blessed, as you give God an opportunity to multiply the seeds you have sown. This does not, by any stretch

44

of the imagination, mean that receiving is bad either. It just means that when you are a giver, you tend to receive more on the other end. Women, in particular, were designed to give. God made women "givers of life." That also means women bring life to dead situations for family, friends, church, and at the workplace.

We will discover that whatever God has assigned to the hands of a man, a woman is the giver of life to it. Giving is very powerful. When we give of ourselves, we build an armory of resources, of people, places, and things. When we are givers, we give ourselves the opportunity for self-growth, expansion, and personal enhancement. In the same way, we give unto others only to enrich them in every way that is a blessing to them and to others. Ultimately, the very act of giving makes us excited. It is no wonder that when a woman ceases to give life, many times she will find herself succumbing to her lower life. She becomes hard, brittle, and bitter. She is easily provoked and irritated and becomes miserable and lacking in flexibility. She starts to lose her softness as a woman! In the scripture in Mark chapter 11, verse 14 (NIV), Jesus cursed a fig tree thus because it was barren. "Then he said to the tree, 'May no one ever eat fruit from you again.'" From that point, the fig tree withered away and did not produce life or fruit again. That is what happens to you when you draw back from being a giver because you have suffered hurt or disappointment. You wither away in the spirit, and you stop your blessings from coming to you. So simply continue giving for you will never be able to count the rewards. "Do not repay evil with evil or insult with insult. On the contrary, repay evil with blessing, because to this you were called so that you may inherit a blessing" (1 Peter 3:9, NIV).

The third and final weapon for restoration is love. The very popular story of Ike and Tina Turner comes to mind. According to the press, Ike Turner was a very abusive husband. When Tina, his wife, eventually summoned sufficient strength to take a courageous and dignified exit from that horrific situation, she wrote a song to complement her departure and titled it "What's Love Got to Do With It?" Tina began evangelizing to any and every woman who cared to listen to her. In all, she appeared to be sending a message of caution to women, but it was also clear that her message was one borne out of all the hurt and pain she had suffered. Her bitter message was to not look for love in your relationships because it is not worth the effort. Love is overly rated and there are other things in a relationship that are more important than love. If love is not the basis of a relationship, then what is? Can an authentic relationship be sustained in any other means? In other words, Love's value is of little reward to the giver. Her message came at a time when societal ills were at their inglorious height, and still are. I believe this is all because we have lost our fundamental thread of compassion and our love for humanity. Because of our grave deceit and our divisive ways, we have arrived at that unfortunate and rather sorry pass where we plaintively cry out, "What's love got to do with it?" I respond with an emphatic "Everything!" Love has everything to do with it! Love still works! In the scripture in 1 Corinthians chapter 13, verse 8 (NIV), it says, "Love never fails…" It is true. Love is still your greatest weapon. Love still works. Love is contagious and infectious. Love is sacrificing and forgiving. Love is a healer and a transformer. Love is God and God is love.

Love, indeed, and in truth, still works! The tragic fact is that many of us offer only mere tokens of love, or we make little deposits here and there because of our misguided belief that to love is a risky venture. We are almost afraid to love. But to love is to walk in the ministry of reconciliation that Jesus called us to, as we can see from the scripture in 2 Corinthians chapter 5, verses 17 through 21 (NIV):

> Therefore, if anyone is in Christ, the new creation has come. The old has gone, the new is here! All this is from God, who reconciled us to himself through Christ and gave us the ministry of reconciliation: that God was reconciling the world to himself in Christ, not counting people's sins against them. And he has committed to us the message of reconciliation. We are therefore Christ's ambassadors, as though God were making his appeal through us. We implore you on Christ's behalf: Be reconciled to God. God made

him who had no sin to be sin for us, so that in
him we might become the righteousness of God.

In summation, whatever you need is in love. It is also in God because God is love. Paul said, "And now these three remain: faith, hope and love. But the greatest of these is love." Actually, it is not only that love is everything; love is also all that ultimately matters. This is because love is the highest and the most luminous state anyone can possibly hope to achieve for love truly conquers all. It breaks down any and all perceived barriers between us all. There is no greater power, in heaven or on earth, than love. This should hardly come as a surprise. In its highest nature, love is the force we recognize as the will of God. We are all great civil engineers. The only tragedy in this fact is that we continually employ our engineering skills to erect walls of discord and disharmony between ourselves. Rather, we should all commit to building bridges of love between one another's hearts. That is why love is the greatest challenge for humanity as a whole. We each have an individual mission. We all have a collective mission. That mission is to continue to spread this love. That love should be the foundation of all we do and say. The world will know God's people by their humility, giving spirit and that love.

On a final note, the Bible declares that "the Just shall live by Faith." It also says that "without Faith it is impossible to please God." Whatever the Bible says is not of faith is sin. We also know that faith without works is dead, and that faith works by love!

That means God is taking us right back to love through the working of our faith; and Love is always the high road. Amen.

CHAPTER 7

Love Me More Than These?

Jesus said to Simon Peter, "Simon son of John, do you love me more than these?" "Yes, Lord," he said, "you know that I love you.
—John 21:15 (NIV)

I recall that I was still on the rough and twisting road to the place of healing, where I would regulate my heart, such that I could rid my soul and spirit of the bitterness and resentment that were the cancerous symptoms of the deep-seated unforgiveness that seemed to have built a nest in my soul. The Lord spoke to me again. As usual, His voice came loud and clear. "Love me more than these?" Well, I was well aware of the scripture in which those very words were uttered by Jesus, but I did not say a word. I remained silent because I knew God well enough to expect that if He chose to do so, He would lay further emphasis on His question. The Lord asked me that question again. "Love me more than these?" Frankly, I can't quite remember if I responded like Simon did: "Yes, I love you, Lord" or if I still remained silent. One thing was, however, certain. I wasn't about to allow the Lord to make me fall into His trap the way Peter did! As if I could fool God. I could no more fool God than Peter did. However, I remained silent and turned my attention to my upcoming preaching engagement.

One day, a few weeks later, as I was driving down the street, I found myself worshipping God. I distinctly recall my words. I said, "I love you, Lord." At that precise moment, I felt a very tender current course through my heart and my being. Once more, I felt tender all over, and it seemed that all the bitterness and the anger that had consumed me for so long was seeping out of my every pore in a raging current of relief. In those moments of release, I felt the totality of the warmth of the love of God. I was so overwhelmed with emotion that crying unto the Lord, I said, "I love you, Lord." His presence was truly with me in a special way, for He spoke back to me. He said, "Love me more than these?" My spirit was calm as I finally prepared to fully understand God's question, "Love me more than these?"

The Lord spoke to my spirit, "You can't love ME and hold these ugly works in your heart. You can't love ME while harboring a spirit of unforgiveness. You cannot love me purely while holding onto anger and bitterness. When you can love me more than these, then you are loving ME."

What, in essence, was God trying to tell me? God was saying that love and bitterness cannot coexist in the life of a child of His. He was saying that love and unforgiveness cannot dwell in the same place. He was saying that love and hatred cannot operate in the same environment. Let us visit the scientific world of physics for an instant. There are some laws of physics that roughly state that certain things cannot occupy the same space at the same time. Perhaps an expedient example of this is Pauli's Exclusion Principle that says two electrons cannot occupy the same state in a molecular orbital. To simplify an already complex scientific concept, one electron will have to give way for the other. To relate it with biblical precept, you will have to revile one and then cling to the other. As the scripture in Luke chapter 16, verse 13 (NIV) puts it, "No one can serve two masters. Either you will hate the one and love the other, or you will be devoted to the one and despise the other." In other words, the Spirit of the Lord was saying to my spirit that there is no tragedy, crisis or disappointment that should ever be placed above, or cover over his love working through us to others.

It is what we dwell upon that expands in our life. That is why the emotions that can draw us away from the love of God, such as anger, resentment, and unforgiveness, can distract us in our love walk with Him. Unforgiveness, in particular, is like a malignant cancer.

Now, I talk a lot about unforgiveness in this book because the reality of its potency (venom) is hidden many times from the conscious mind. Like cancer, it seldom stays stagnant. It multiplies to destroy the soul in much the same way that cancer cells multiply to destroy the body. When the space that is supposed to be occupied by love is occupied by unforgiveness, unforgiveness starts to grow to occupy that space and gradually forces love out. Yet it is also true that nature does not particularly like a vacuum.

According to the ancient philosopher, Aristotle, "Nature abhors a vacuum." Aristotle's conclusion was based on the observation that nature requires every space to be filled with something, no matter what that thing is. The same principle is at work in our spiritual lives. If we refuse to allow our inner space to be filled with love, we leave room for its occupation by the killers of our soul, like anger, resentment, and unforgiveness. The funny thing is that, even if we rid ourselves of these negative emotions and do not immediately start to replace them with thoughts of love, we are still leaving space for occupation by unwholesome emotions. Yes, our inner space cannot be left void. The spiritually idle mind is the devil's workshop. We must keep it working in, and for love. Every attempt to get rid of unloving thoughts and emotions creates a vacuum in our souls. As soon as we empty ourselves of one, if we do not immediately fill ourselves with love, another can move in to take its place, and we end up just as bad or worse than when we started. Thinking about vacuums helps us to understand the importance of what Paul told the Ephesians in chapter 3, verse 19 (NIV), when he prayed that Christ would dwell in their hearts through faith, and that they would "know the Love of Christ, that they may be filled with all the fullness of God."

The only permanent solution to the problem of unforgiveness in our lives is to replace it with love, so as to fill the vacuum. The more we are filled with love, the less room we leave for any evil emotion.

The medical world has a term called space-occupying lesion. In the neurological world of medicine, space-occupying lesions are growths within the skull, which presents with common symptoms and signs. By far the commonest space-occupying lesions are brain tumors, either original tumors or deposits that result from tumors elsewhere in the body. When love is your own space-occupying lesion, it is harmless and of great benefit to you. However, when your space-occupying lesion is resentment, then you have a problem because what you have is a cancer of the soul that will eventually grow and consume you the way cancer cells grow to consume the body.

But how can we grow in right thought so that we can finally occupy our minds with thoughts of God's love? Our thoughts are very powerful, and they can ultimately define the quality of our spiritual life. In the scripture in Philippians chapter 4, verse 8 (NIV), Paul says, "Finally, brothers and sisters, whatever is true, whatever is noble, whatever is right, whatever is pure, whatever is lovely, whatever is admirable; if anything is excellent or praiseworthy, think about such things." Think! Think! Think!

You see, as believers, we are to "think about these things." The more we think about these things, the more we disallow the enemy from coming to set up residence in our minds. While God guards our hearts, we are also commanded to focus on those things that please God. At the same time, we are commanded to live according to God's ways. He does His work, yet He gives us work to do. We are called to trust in the Lord yet also to serve the Lord.

Yes. We must focus on and fill our mind with that which is true. The opposite of true is lie. Truth is fixed. Truth is objective and not subjective. Some people spuriously argue that truth can be relative. It is absurd to state that the truth can be flexible or subjective. Something is either true or untrue. God's natural order is one of love, and His love is the truth. The Bible is God's Word. The Bible is truth. It is called "the Word of Truth." As the scripture in John chapter 1, verse 1 (NIV) says, "In the beginning was the Word, and the Word was with God, and the Word was God." Jesus Himself is truth. He says in John chapter 14, verse 6 (NIV), "I am the way and the truth and the life. No one comes to the Father except through me." If you immerse yourself in the Word of God, you cannot help but continually think about truth. The Bible says those who meditate day and night on God's Word will be like trees planted by streams of water, which yields its fruit in season and whose leaf does not wither, and whatever they do prospers. Since by its very nature the mind of God is true, noble, right, pure, lovely, and admirable, and since His mind is revealed in His Word, those who meditate on Scripture day and night will increasingly have minds with the same qualities. That kind of thinking leaves no space for negative or unproductive thoughts.

Nobility is having and displaying personal qualities that people admire, such as honesty, generosity, and courage. We know nobility when we see it. We see it in the husband who gallantly sticks by his wife's side as she goes through the pains of cancer chemotherapy. We see it in the man who returns a lost wallet to the lost-and-found office. Whatever we do, integrity should always be at the back of our mind. Whatever happens, we should conduct ourselves in a manner worthy of the Gospel of Christ. In earlier days, multimillion-dollar deals were sealed with a handshake, for, in those days, a person's word was his bond. That is seldom the case these days. But that is how it should be among Christians. We should fill our minds only with thoughts of integrity.

God's way of love recognizes that there is right and there is wrong. Right is correct. Wrong is incorrect. Love, the true love, which derives from God Himself, is right. Hate is wrong. Right stems from truth and grace. Wrong comes from enmity and hatred. Right is to forgive others so that we may be forgiven. Wrong is to resent, begrudge, and refuse to acquiesce to what you know is right. Right comes from God the Father. Wrong comes from the father of lies, the devil.

The love of God is pure. Pure is that which is free from what weakens or pollutes, and it contains nothing that does not properly belong. Fidelity to one's spouse and the marriage bed is pure. Adultery is impure. True marriage is pure. Contentment is pure. Covetousness is impure. Selfishness in a marriage is impure. Jesus is pure. True Christianity is pure. It is when we insist on thinking pure thoughts that we can disallow impure thoughts from taking the space of our minds. We also need to relate love with lovely. Lovely is defined as "attractive or beautiful, especially in a graceful way." Outward beauty can be lovely. However, the inward beauty that derives from the Holy

Spirit is always lovely. God's nature, which is love, is lovely. His creation and created order are lovely. What about all that is admirable? That which is admirable inspires approval and reverence. The whole of God's creation is admirable. God is worthy of infinite wonder, praise, and worship. It is when we start to admire things that fall short of what is admirable in the context of God's love and we start to think about such things that we wrongfully occupy the space that was meant for His love.

What about excellent thoughts? Excellence refers to something of extremely high quality. We are told to not only think about that which is excellent, but to strive for excellence in all we do. We also know excellence when we see it. That is why the Bible admonishes us that whatever our hands find to do, we should do it with all our might.

Finally, our thoughts should be praiseworthy. They should be deserving and be worthy of praise. Anything that is true, noble, right, pure, lovely, admirable, and excellent is also praiseworthy. These are the basis of the thoughts we should continually entertain in our minds. Why is this so? Jesus is true. Jesus is noble. Jesus is right. Jesus is pure. Jesus is lovely. Jesus is admirable. Jesus is excellent and, finally, and perhaps most importantly, Jesus is infinitely praiseworthy.

I had been given a baptism in God's love once again, and I was truly loving God back. My new realization was that when you allow the love of God to occupy every corner of your heart (in different measures, of course, because it is always a work in progress), you are free to live a life without restraints, limitations, and people's opinions. It is a walk of true spiritual freedom and you will experience God's peace, which exceeds anything the soul can understand. The beauty of it all is that God's peace will guard your heart and mind as you live in Christ Jesus, and He will continually take you to deeper levels of truths.

CHAPTER 8

Grief in Love

Brothers and sisters, we do not want you to be unin-
formed about those who sleep in death, so that you do
not grieve like the rest of mankind, who have no hope.
—1 Thessalonians 4:13 (NIV)

When an elderly person dies, we do feel sad, and we express it. At the same time, however, we may often feel a certain relief or the pangs and pains of old age. On the other hand, when the cold hands of death snatches someone we love, and perhaps in some tragic manner, for that matter, long before what we perceive to be their appointed time, we tend to experience a sense of profound pain that sometimes borders on the unbearable. We hear from psychologists that the worst pain in life is the loss of one's own child. Most of us would agree to this. Grief, an emotion of intense sorrow, is the term for this sort of psychic pain. It is obviously the price we pay for "love," and the closer the bond, the deeper the hurt that we feel at the loss of the loved one. The pertinent question now becomes "What is the place of grief in the life of a believer?" The Bible certainly does not tell us not to grieve, but to grieve like people to whom the Lord has given a certain hope of heaven. As it says in the scripture of Matthew chapter 5, verse 4 (NIV), "Blessed are those who mourn, for they shall be comforted."

My ninety-year-old aunt passed on about 9:00 a.m. on the eve of the New Year in 2016. She was very dear to me and very much like another mother. She was my mother's last living sibling. She was sweet and kind and was truly like a second mother to me. You would never hear a critical word from her mouth.

Then on January 4, 2017, my niece called me about 7:00 a.m., but I was praying on our church's conference line. I heard the interrupting call, but I thought it was my daughter L'Tanya. I had spoken with her only the night before and had jokingly told her not to call me early the next morning. It was when I got off the conference line that I saw it was a call from my niece. I called her. She dropped the devastating news. Her brother had passed on. It felt as if someone had punched me in the stomach with all their might. I screamed and cried. It affected me even more than the heartbreaking news of my dear aunt's passage. Why?

My nephew had been a fine young man with a bright future ahead of him. He had also been a loving father, as his children adored him and would be all over him whenever he was around them. My nephew was kind and confident. He was a very caring man and loved and respected his mother and sister. I once observed a conversation between him and his mother, in which he called for some personal advice. I had found it very touching that even at twenty-five, he still valued his mother's wisdom and counsel. I also once observed an equally inspiring business interaction between him and his uncle. I learned so much from my nephew. He was simply a stand-up guy, who, when and if he trusted you, you were certain that you had a faithful friend or family member. He was truly a good man. However, in the final analysis, whether you lost your ninety-year-old aunt or your twenty-five-year-old son, you end up hurting. You grieve. And you may grieve rather badly. Some people will tell you that you should not show your grief, especially if you are a Christian. The practical point such people may be easily overlooking is that grief is the way we say to our loved ones, "I love you, and I miss you. You were special. No one will ever take your place. I am sorry that I won't see you until we meet again in heaven."

But then, how are we supposed to grieve? Join me and take a look at the scripture in Hebrews chapter 9, verse 27 (NIV): "Just as people are destined to die once, and after that to face judgment." What this tells us is that from the day we make our entrance into this world, our irrevocable destiny is to die. It is an unavoidable destiny. From dust we came, and to dust we must, and will, return.

Having established that fact, I think the first thing we have to accept is that grief, by its very nature, is a very complex emotion. That is not surprising. Any emotion that is a reflection of man's fundamental vulnerability as a mere mortal will necessarily be quite complex. Because of this, there are many facets to the complexity called grief. That is why we should avoid the temptation of stereotyping people and trying to squeeze them into our own perception of how one should or should not grieve. We all grieve in different ways, and that should be quite all right. Clearly, also, there are progressive stages to grieving, and they may not necessarily come in the same order for everyone, with your stages coming in a sequence that is the exact opposite of mine. To cap it all, there is an ever-present confusion, especially for Christians. We are at a loss as to how to act in our period of grief. We are torn apart by conflicting emotions. We have faith that God cares, and that He is in control, yet in the same agonizing instant, we are tortured by feelings of doubt that He doesn't care or really in control. We feel that it is perfectly all right to cry, but we are also filled with dread that others might see it as a lack of faith. We are rejoicing that our loved one is with God, yet we wish they were still here with us. We are in such a turmoil that we wish we could explode emotionally. We are caught up in between the tense grip of holding ourselves together or just letting ourselves go!

Job said, "The Lord gives, and the Lord takes away. Blessed be the name of the Lord." Although Job would later be quoted verbatim anytime someone passed on in Christendom, the reality was that he actually exploded emotionally and theologically, as we can see in Job chapter 3 (NIV), when his children and everything that was precious to him was taken away from him. In our excursion through the book of Job, we will see that it wasn't until forty chapters later that he managed to compose himself and collect himself together again to declare his faith in God.

Paradoxically, however, we somehow and finally reach, not the end of hurting itself, but, thankfully, the end of the unbearable side to the hurt. Indeed, we wake up one day, and we discover that we seem to have managed to attain some semblance of normalcy. What does this tell us? I think the inference we can draw is that the only hope available to us in times of dark despair and depression is that "it will pass." At the instant of the beginning of the agony, we do not believe it will pass. But it will. This too shall pass. Seemingly good or seemingly bad, nothing lasts forever. Everything will pass. That is not only an immutable law of the human experience, but also one of unerring exactitude. No matter the harrowing or seemingly terrible experience you may be subjected to, it will surely pass. The only thing that will remain, unchanging, is our Creator and our Lord. At that point of acute distress, we do not think life is worth living, but it is. We do not think we can go on, but we can. Time is the great healer, not necessarily of "hurt," but "unbearable hurt." That is why you have to lean on Jesus to get you through the dark times. He can help you grow on to a richer and fuller life.

So after all is said and done, how should we grieve? The answer to this all-important question is: with gratitude to God. This sounds so strange, and perhaps too simplistic, *maybe unempathetic*, doesn't it? Yes, with gratitude to God. Yes, it sounds very strange and impractical, but you have to trust God that His love for you goes beyond anything we experience, and which we believe has impacted us so negatively in our loss. Your assignment will be to trust God that His love goes much deeper than the pain you are feeling right now. You have to trust that God has no intention whatsoever of hurting you, and while you may not possess that full understanding, since you may not be able to trace His hand right now, you will have trust in His love for you.

On a practical note, as you grieve, the healthiest thing is to remember the good times you had with the loved one that just passed. Then, remain in a state of gratitude for the friends and family you still have. The next thing is to practice forgiveness. We must forgive ourselves for not being perfect. Give yourself a break! Who among us can look at a coffin without saying, "O God, why did I do this to this person?" or "Why didn't I do this for this person?" Each one of us has done and said things that we later regret. Accept God's forgiveness, and then accept the forgiveness of your loved one. They were not perfect either. Also, you will need to get rid of any guilt you might feel for getting on with your life. You will need to rid yourself of the guilt of being happy again when life begins to take on a new meaning for you, as it eventually will.

We often feel we owe it to our loved one to remain interminably miserable. But that, too, is an insult to your beloved. Life must continue. You owe it to yourself and your loved one to continue in your own love walk with God, and with as much joy as you can muster, seizing each new day with a gladness of heart that celebrates God's prescription that you should rejoice and be glad in the day, for it is the day that the Lord has made.

We should also grieve by trusting. We have to repose sufficient faith in God to be honest and to believe there is some answer or purpose to the mystery of our existence even though we may never know it until we get to heaven. We must go on with God, serving Him even while our questions remain unanswered.

For Scottish minister and professor of theology, Pastor Thomas Chalmers, his wife's death at a relatively young age was a blow that sorely tasked his calling as minister of God's Word. In his first sermon after her death, he asked, "Should I turn away from God? In heaven's name, where could I go?" It is all right to question God; the problem is He does not usually answer at times like this. This is where faith comes in. This classic poem by Ella Wheeler Wilcox is soothing balm for the grieving soul:

> I will not doubt, though all my ships at sea;
> Come drifting home, with broken masts and sails;
> I shall believe the Hand which never fails;
> For seeming evil, worked good for me,
> And though I weep because the sails are battered
> Still will I cry, while my best hopes lie shattered?
> I trust in thee.

The poignant truth is that there is ministry in the passing of your beloved. Through this ministry of grace, you are called by God to carry on the legacy. Don't let it die.

Death has a great way of making us reevaluate life and has the equally great value of teaching us what is really important in life. This is the reason why, although we can grieve, we should not do so as if we have no hope. Rather, we should keep hope alive.

I will share another lesson that we can learn from the transition of a loved one. That lesson can be found in this true story. In the story, my cousin shared with me a beautiful moment she had with her mother just before she went home to be with the Lord. As she shared her story, I couldn't help thinking that in truth, blindness is a metaphor for a closed mind. My cousin told me that her mother's eyes were cloudy and covered over with a film. Of course, we all know that would make it difficult for her mother to see clearly. Eyes are the window to the soul. But although your eyes might be the proverbial window to the soul, they are also a clear window to your health, and the amount of information they can reveal is simply astonishing.

It is little wonder that the scripture in Matthew chapter 6, verse 22 (NIV) says, "The eye is the lamp of the body. If your eyes are healthy, your whole body will be full of light." Fully more than thirty medical ailments display eye symptoms. That is why eye doctors, called ophthalmologists, are frequently among the first you consult to sort out certain problems. An internal study of 120,000 patients by the insurance company, Vision Care, found that an eye examination was the first predictor of 34% of diabetes cases, 39% of cases of high blood pressure, and a shocking 62% of cases of high blood cholesterol level. Those are medical implications. There are also spiritual implications concerning your eyes. Let us go to the story of how the disciples had forgotten to bring bread, except for the one loaf they had with them on the boat.

Jesus was disappointed with their response. We see His disappointment in Mark 8:17–19 (NIV):

> Jesus asked them: "Why are you talking about having no bread? Do you still not see or understand? Are your hearts hardened? Do you have eyes but fail to see, and ears but fail to hear? And don't you remember? When I broke the five

loaves for the five thousand, how many basket-
fuls of pieces did you pick up?" "Twelve," they
replied.

Jesus was disappointed because their response showed they
did not remember. They did not believe that Jesus was the miracle
worker, and that there is nothing impossible with Jesus.

Circumstances, pain, and disappointments will sometimes
color the truth, but the truth will always remain the truth. The disciples were like we are today. When tragedy strikes, we forget that
God remains the same God. You must always remember those good
works that God had previously done in your life. They will help you
to trust in Him to help you solve the next problem in your life. Even
in the painful loss of your loved one, you have to trust in Him. God
is sovereign. He does what He wants, when He wants, and how He
wants. You should keep a long memory for His mercies and a short
one for your failures.

But what keeps us from seeing clearly? The first is pride and
defective faith. In the scripture in Mark chapter 8, verse 15 (NIV),
Jesus said, "Be careful. Watch out for the yeast of the Pharisees and
that of Herod." Jesus was warning on pride and defective faith. Yeast,
or leaven, is here used to symbolize something with a dangerously
pervasive influence. As we all know, yeast allows bread to swell up,
and the bigger it becomes, the hotter the air that is engulfing it.
In other words, Jesus is warning them to be aware of their sphere
of influence. He was admonishing them not to be deceived by the
world, but to remain sober-minded so that their vision would not
be affected. However, Luke chapter 12, verse 1 (NIV) explains that
the leaven of the Pharisees is hypocrisy. The leaven of Herod may be
the influence of the Herodians, which was a spirit of worldliness and
an infectious secularism. Hypocrisy is playacting. Is your life just a
playact or a game?

The second thing that keeps us from seeing clearly is short-term
thinking or small-mindedness. We are all familiar with the popular saying "Great minds discuss ideas; average minds discuss events;
small minds discuss people." The Bible tells us that the disciples

"discussed this with one another and said, it is because we have no bread." The disciples did not perceive what He meant by the leaven. The blindness of the Pharisees does not surprise us in the least. But why were His disciples equally so blind? Like Israel of old, the disciples saw His acts but failed to understand His ways. That is the problem with many confessed believers. They seem to know all about God's acts. They can recognize the works of God. They will give Him all the praise and glory. They are thankful for answered prayers. Despite all these, however, they remain ignorant of His ways. They don't know His heart. They don't know His word. There really isn't any true relationship between them and God. So we should truly ask God for spiritual insight. This leads me to my final point. And it is about defective devotion.

When we look further into the scripture in Mark chapter 8 (NIV), we can see Jesus addressing His disciples on their lack of faith and trust in Him. Look at Peter, for instance. In one minute, Peter is inspired from heaven, and in the next minute, his tongue is ignited from hell. Peter saw only shame in the cross, but Jesus saw glory. Peter saw defeat, but Jesus saw great victory. We should never be ashamed to be His disciple. Your beloved mother is with the Lord, but God has not forsaken you. Jesus can heal your vision, and He does so in three ways. Your focus gets sharper. Your perspective gets larger. Your vision gets clearer.

I now return to my cousin sharing that at the point of her mother's transition to her heavenly home, she looked into her mother's eyes, and they were so unclear. The white of her eyes were gray and cloudy, with a tinge of red. The pupils of her eyes had a film over them, which we can assume made it difficult for her to see clearly, if at all. But when she took her last breath and as she transitioned to heaven, her eyes changed right in front of her daughter. The white of her eyes became white and clear. Her pupils became clear, black, and bright. It was as if God was giving a clear sign that it was well with her soul. Her mother, at her last moment on this earth, could see clearly. She could see clearly because she had seen the King.

Clear up your vision so that you can see clearly. There is no age, ethnicity, talent, or ministry that positions us in an exclusive class or an exclusive category that guarantees our place in heaven. But we will all stand before God one day and will have to answer the question: "Did you make me your Lord and the Savior of your life?"

"What did you do with the life I gave you?" It is your answer to that final question that will determine whether your sojourn on this earthly plane had been worth all the trouble. To Him be all the glory. Amen.

CHAPTER 9

The Crown of Pride

In that day the Lord Almighty will be a glorious crown,
a beautiful wreath for the remnant of his people.
—Isaiah 28:5 (NIV)

It was truly a land of milk and honey. It was a land of plenty, and it was a land that displayed God's abundance at its most lavish. Even the name of the tribe of Ephraim depicted "doubled fruitfulness," for "God had made him fruitful in the land of his affliction." That the name derived from fruitfulness was not surprising since the soil was extraordinarily fertile, bearing products, both in lavish abundance and in the form of the very best of their kind. It was a land of great and lush valleys that were covered with corn and vines. The city of Samaria, which was on a hill, was situated right at the head of these luxuriant valleys. It was a rich and pleasant country, and in those days, the whole of Canaan could only have been correctly described as "the Garden of the Lord." As the land that was promised the Israelites, it depicted nothing but the glory of a land blessed by God.

But their extremely good fortune was also the source of their tragic fate. The tragedy of their fate laid in the wrong use they made of their plenitude. What God had given them to serve Him and to glorify His name before all nations became perverted and abused, as they now turned round to make it food and fuel for their lust. They became puffed up with pride by their possessions. What was placed at their disposal for their own good would later turn out to be the cause of their downfall.

God sent Isaiah to them. Isaiah made his first public appearance as the divinely-inspired prophet in the year of Uzziah's affliction with leprosy, and he ministered to the people for about ninety years, during the reigns of kings Uzziah, Jotham, Ahaz, and Hezekiah. At a time when idolatry seemed to be taking hold in the land, Isaiah had seen the fall of the kingdom of Israel and the rise of a new empire called Assyria. Isaiah brought to king and people the message of the holiness of God. He screamed himself hoarse, preaching justice and charity at a time when the morals of the people had attained an all-time low.

> And I heard the voice of God, saying: "Whom shall I send, and who will go for us?" And I said: "Here am I; send me." And God replied: "Go, say unto this people; Ye hear indeed, but understand not; ye see indeed, but know not." (Isaiah 6:9, NIV)

> And Isaiah now asked God, "How long, oh Lord, will the people remain obstinate?" And God replied: "Until their cities be left waste without inhabitants, and houses without men, and the land be made desolate as a wilderness. Till God will have removed the men far away, and there will be great desolation in the midst of the land." (Isaiah 6:12, NIV)

Isaiah ran around barefoot and naked for three years, proclaiming the Word of God. He warned of the coming judgment of God upon Israel for their sins. Soon after, his prophecies came to pass, and Assyria carried Jordan, the ten tribes, into captivity and laid their entire country to waste and desolation. Isaiah was distressed because although great devastation was prophesied, Jerusalem was celebrating instead of mourning. The people reinforced the city walls and built water reservoirs in preparation for the war they knew was inevitable. In all these, they refused to acknowledge God and did not seek His face and help. At that time, Israelites had become rather cocky about their great city, Jerusalem, believing that God would never allow it to fall into enemy hands. Pride had taken over the Israelites. Pride had become a sin that generally prevailed among them, and finally, Isaiah boldly proclaimed a verdict of woe unto him who insisted on wearing the crown of pride. As the prophet Isaiah said in the book of Isaiah, chapter 28, verse 1 (NIV), "Woe to the crown of pride, to the drunkards of Ephraim, whose glorious beauty is a fading flower, which are on the head of the fat valleys of them that are overcome with wine!"

When men become proud, it assumes the grandeur of a crown on their head. This is because he that is proud begins to think of himself as great as a king. But woe unto those who exalt themselves for they shall be abased. Their pride is the preface to the destruction that awaits them, as this chapter suggests. In other words, there are also crowns of glory. These are crowns that reflect the glory of man and crowns that reflect the glory of God. But men have, instead, chosen to place the crown of pride on their heads.

That crown of man that is rooted in pride is not a new story. In Genesis chapter 11 (NIV), we see a prototype of the church, in which the people conspired to build a tower, the Tower of Babel, that would reach up to the heavens. God was quick to spot the conspiracy and swiftly came down to cause confusion among them by putting different languages on their tongues, disallowing them to further understand one another, effectively putting paid to their grandiose plans. What was man trying to do with the Tower of Babel? He wanted to build a name for himself, when his obligation was supposed to be building up God's name.

Pride can become intoxicating. Men become so drunk on the wine of their self-importance and get so filled with pride that they no longer know when they are sinning against God. What pride does to us is pathetic. Pride makes you go underground and hide. As a result of pride, we hide in building projects. We hide in keeping busy, conveniently forgetting that there is more to Christianity besides building buildings. We totally forget about the business of building people. That was what was wrong with the people of God in those times. They built walls and water reservoirs to prepare for war but did not turn to God for help because of their arrogant assumption that God would never allow their city of Jerusalem to fall into enemy hands. Pride had become a prevalent sin amongst them, and that was why the prophet Isaiah boldly proclaimed, "Woe to the crown of pride."

There are crowns that men wear that are an antithesis to the love of God. There are crowns men have placed on their heads that operate in complete contradiction to what the Word of God declares. In other words, there is no place for ego in the kingdom of God. Let us, for the purpose of this chapter's message, consider "EGO" as an acronym for "Erasing God Out." There is nothing on this earth as strong or as ugly as pride. Pride reeks of the unspoken message that "I am at the center of my life, and I am in total control, and all my accomplishments are my glory!" Pride resides at the other end of the spectrum and very far away from humility.

How does God view pride? Only His own Word can give us an accurate clue, and two scriptures immediately come to mind. The first is James chapter 4, verse 6 (NIV), which says, "God resists the proud, but gives grace to the humble" while the second is Proverbs chapter 6, verses 16 and 17 (NIV), which say, "There are six things the Lord hates; seven that are detestable to him: haughty eyes, a lying tongue, hands that shed innocent blood."

Firmly rooted in pride is the spirit of Jezebel. In the book of Kings in the Bible, Jezebel was the queen who incited her husband, King Ahab, to abandon the worship of God and encourage the worship of the idol Baal instead. Jezebel persecuted the prophets of God and fabricated evidence of blasphemy against an innocent landowner who had refused to sell his property to King Ahab, causing the landowner to be put to death. For these transgressions against the God and the people of Israel, Jezebel met a gruesome death. She was thrown out of a window by members of her own court retinue, and her corpse was left out in the open fields to be eaten by stray dogs.

I believe Jezebel has crept into the church and established residence therein. Admittedly, everyone has character flaws and blind spots, but we now find several characteristics of a Jezebel spirit that work in unholy concert with pride. Jezebel is a spirit, but it has found access into the church through uncrucified flesh. Jezebel, the spirit of control, has attempted to cripple the church of God. In the strictest term of usage, we need to know that Jezebel is not a person, and that it is not restricted to either sex. Also, although it is often perceived as being more prevalent in women, it actually works its way up to the headship. It attaches itself to people of influence and power. Jezebel is a product of the flesh that opens the door to an evil spirit for it to gain easy access. Its strategy is to operate through a person who attempts to exert control by the use of manipulative, domineering, and intimidating tactics. The name Jezebel specifically means "without dwelling or habitation." This is absolutely true of its nature. It is an independent spirit. It cohabits with no one. It is committed to no one except to its own self-will. Indeed, a true way of depicting Jezebel is to describe it as the worship of self-will, which is obviously the exact antithesis of God's love, agape love. The clear battle line that the Jezebel spirit draws is with people. The spirit desires to rule and control the people of God. If we do not insist on being people of resolute decision, we will fall under the spell of the Jezebel spirit. The perfect description of her agenda is that it exalts position over character. It is true that Jezebel lays a pretentious claim to religion, but what she does is to wield her false power against the true prophetic flow of God. She hates the prophets and all of prophetic ministry. Specifically, she harbors a special hatred for repentance, humility, and intercessory prayer because they destroy her strongholds of stubbornness and pride.

Certain traits are the hallmark of the Jezebel spirit. One is by no means declaring that as soon as someone has one or two of these characteristics, the person should be categorized as a person with a Jezebel spirit. However, when a number of these traits are evident in a person, then you are probably dealing with both the Jezebel spirit and the personality of a Jezebel. Such a person never admits guilt or wrongdoing, and because true repentance is anathema to him, and we are using the masculine here to depict both genders, the question of apologizing never arises. He will also insist on taking the credit for any and everything, even in the face of no contribution to the common cause.

Being a totally manipulative and coldly calculating person, he will use people to accomplish his own agenda at will in a most self-centered and selfish manner. Worse, being someone who aims to exert absolute control over people and situations, he will callously withhold crucial information from others, just so as to have the upper hand in all encounters. Curiously, he always seems to be the first to be in the possession of such information and will do all in his power to sequester it to himself as a leverage for power over others. Sincerity being so far from him, he will often talk in a confused and incoherent manner, jumping from one subject to the next in a space of just five minutes. Of course, in any verbal encounter, you would find him doing all the talking, as he is unable to receive input from anyone, and all his interactions are invariably one-sided. He will volunteer for any assignment under the sun, simply to establish control and bring everything under his own pervasive sphere of influence. He will lie, not only at will, but convincingly.

The person who has been completely taken over by the spirit of Jezebel will intentionally ignore those who are in disagreement with his views, and this is particularly seen in leaders who wish to oppress their followers. Naturally, he is never inclined to give credit to anyone who doesn't agree with his ideas or who does not show deep gratitude for his ill-motivated goodwill. On his own part, and quite hypocritically, he is unable to utter the words "Thank you" for any kindness or good deed shown him. He will criticize anyone at the drop of a hat but is generous in complimenting those who agree with him. Upstaging and one-upmanship are his stock in trade. A typical controller tends to fall back on spirituality as a platitude to explain away his personal problems, using God as convenient crutch at such times. His pushy and domineering nature relegates you to the position of someone who is incapable of making sense out of the most elementary issue, and so you cannot think independently.

Often, many who operate with a spirit of control also possess a clairvoyant spirit. Clairvoyance may be defined as the power to perceive things that are out of the range of the human senses. A Jezebel appears to receive some form of supernatural help in knowing and sensing information beforehand. If he ends up using this against you, he may say something like, "I can't tell you how I know this. I just know it." In reality, it is not the Holy Spirit playing itself out here but a clairvoyant or "familiar" spirit. In his role as a power player, he uses the element of surprise with consummate skill, catching you off guard at moments that would otherwise have served you to tremendous advantage. To further inhibit your progress, he will effectively sow seeds of discord between you and your sisters and brothers, belittle your own efforts as being of little or no consequence, and propound half-truths about you to anyone who cares to listen. This is not surprising, as he wishes to remain the center of attention at all times.

Our Jezebel is a very vindictive person. While he sees himself as someone who can do no wrong, he is as vengeful as they come. You can only contradict him at your own peril, and if you do, you automatically become his worst enemy. To ward off suspicion about the dark side to his nature, he may even turn the table on you and attempt to cast you in the light of a Jezebel yourself. In his conceit and in his own eyes, his opinions take on the hue of theology, and he idolizes them, in the process effortlessly insinuating disapproval into any encounter that threatens to give anyone else the freedom to express an opinion. He possesses vaulting ambition, and his credo appears to perennially be "I want what I want, when I want it!" For him, generosity is merely a tool for manipulation since it renders you obligated to Him by receiving His gifts.

A Jezebel is completely independent, and no one appears to have the slightest input in his life. He fraternizes with no one unless such an alliance is to get you to cooperate with his agenda. Religious fervor is also his hallmark. A Jezebel dwells in the local church although even there, you are most unlikely to find him willingly subservient to ecclesiastical authority. He would rather arrogate a position of authority to himself. The funny thing is that the spirit of Jezebel will often go into "hiding" for a length of time, only for a situation to suddenly arise once again, with the spirit taking control and wreaking havoc over other lives.

Is there hope for a person with a spirit of Jezebel? Hopefully, true repentance will eventually come, and only then will the person be delivered from the spirit. What can be done for this person? Those with a Jezebel spirit can be confronted only by someone who will approach them with firmness and love and who will not be afraid of a reaction. Without genuine confrontation, the person will remain in the pattern of control, as it has become a lifestyle, with little or no motivation to change.

God wants us to live higher. The crowns that God wants to see us wear are at complete variance with the crown of pride. He wants to give us a diadem of beauty—a crown of beauty. He wants to crown us with the fruit of the Spirit, and the precious stones embedded in this crown of the fruit of the spirit are those that we find in Galatians chapter 5, verse 25 (NIV), and they are: the crown of love; the crown of joy; the crown of long suffering; the crown of gentleness; the crown of goodness; the crown of meekness; the crown of temperance; and the crown of faith. These crowns belong to those that have become Christ's. For they that are Christ's have crucified the flesh with the affections and the lusts. If we live in the Spirit, let us also walk in the Spirit and not be desirous of vain glory!

What is God saying to us? God is saying to the remnant of His people: "I am going to give you a crown of beauty for your pain, and your suffering. But first take off that crown of pride, so not to give place to the spirit of Jezebel and to create space on your head for my crown of Love."

CHAPTER 10

Skipping Steps

*But let patience have her perfect work that ye may
be perfect, complete, and entire, wanting nothing.*
—James 1:4 (NIV)

To subscribe to the perfect love of God is to align oneself to His perfect process, and His perfect order, in His work in our lives. God is a God of order. God is a God of process. His ways are not our ways. Truly, there is a celestial order to everything under the sun, and just because there seems to be a seemingly interminably long interval between a cause and its effect does not mean that God has gone to sleep, so to speak. You cannot claim to love God if you are not prepared to wait on Him patiently.

In 1995, *Harvard Business Review* first published an article on successful change management written by John P. Kotter, a retired Harvard Business School professor and author of the book *Leading Change: Why Transformation Efforts Fail.* Since that time, Kotter's ideas on executing change have become ingrained in the practices of strong business leaders. When it comes to change management, John Kotter is the most cited author worldwide. His book *Leading Change* was to become an international bestseller. In this book, Kotter describes eight necessary steps for corporate cultural change. He stresses that the eight steps of organizational change need to be implemented in the particular order he had identified to increase the chance of success. Skipping one step, said Kotter, can lead to failure of change. It is amazing, isn't it, how the world takes the principles of

God and give them back to us, as if they owned it in the first place? Professor Kotter's perspective on skipping steps can be summarized with three main points: (1) skipping steps gives the illusion of speed; (2) each phase requires a significant time period; (3) skipping steps never produces long-lasting results. Therefore, we can easily arrive at the wholesome concept that when you have allowed patience to have its way, or complete its work in you, the issue of struggle in any form no longer arises. The reason why some have to struggle so much in life, and in ministry, is that they did not allow patience to accomplish its "perfect work in them."

The scripture in James chapter 1, verse 4 (NIV), says, "But let patience have her perfect work that ye may be perfect complete mature and entire wanting nothing." When you skip steps, you will end up struggling. Quite possibly, you may still obtain your desired results, getting exactly what you wanted, but you will have to struggle to keep it. The panacea is simply not to skip steps. Real transformation is not possible if you avoid a season or phase in your life. That is why the preacher's scripture in Ecclesiastes chapter 3, verse 1 (NIV) explicitly says, "To everything there is a season, and a time to every purpose under the heaven." Note that the scripture clearly says "a time to" and not "a time for."

For centuries, a stream flowed over an outcrop of rock. On the surface, the relationship between stream and rock is simply one of nature playing itself out.

However, their relationship is of far greater significance than that. Put quite simply, theirs is an ecological confrontation. And in this confrontation, the stream is the ultimate winner. It cuts a groove in the rock. Yet the rock is hard, brittle, and strong.

The stream is soft, fluid, and yielding. The stream wins, not by virtue of strength. The stream wins through patience and perseverance.

God's way, which is definitely not our way, is a painstaking process. It takes time to manifest its ultimate objective. Let us examine a couple of examples from the Bible. The scripture in Genesis chapter 4, verses 1 to 15 (NIV) relate the story of the offspring of Adam and Eve—the two siblings, Cain and Abel. In a tragic end to a tale of envy and jealousy, Cain thought he could get to where he wanted to go faster with Abel out of the way. He neither trusted God nor had faith in Him. Earlier, Cain and Abel had offered sacrifices to God. Cain, a farmer, had offered God a portion of his crops as a sacrifice. Abel, on the other hand, being a shepherd, had presented God with the fattest portion of his flock. When it became obvious to Cain that God was more pleased with Abel's sacrifice, Cain killed his brother in a fit of jealousy and anger. When God later asked about Abel's whereabouts from Cain, he shrugged in indifference. With the knowledge that God knew what he had done, he became a marked man and lived in dread of what God would do. It is the same attitude in the lives of Christians today. Because we are rejected today does not mean we will be rejected tomorrow. God is not necessarily just sitting back, waiting to descend on us because we get off track. What God did was to exile Cain from his home and to wander in the land east of Eden. Cain had wanted to skip so many steps and to circumvent His processes to curry God's favor. All of God's ways are judgments. That is the difference between the judgment from the Great White Throne and the judgment of man here on earth.

God judges us today based on our character. Yet in the final analysis, God is into building our character to prepare His church. We are all called to do His work, and some of us will need to do more work than others. What, however, is more important is for us to realize that every season and every period in our lives will require a significant time to yield the desired fruit in God's process. We cannot skip the steps. To love Him is to trust Him and to have faith that, in due season, we shall reap the fruits of our labor.

We see another classic example of man's futile attempt to skip steps in the story of creation, in which Adam and Eve, by indulging in immediate gratification, sought to skip steps and become like God and to possess His wisdom. Let us refresh our memories of the events of that time in the garden of Eden, that unique and lush setting in which He chose to install Man, His greatest and most miraculous creation yet.

One day, this dialogue ensued between Him and Man:

He: I have created this beautiful garden for your aesthetic and culinary delight. Do you like it?

Man: Yes, I do. Thank you very much.

He: Feel quite at liberty to eat from any tree in the garden… Oh, but with the exception of just one. You may not, absolutely may not, eat from the Tree of the Knowledge of Good and Evil, for if and when you do, you will surely die.

Man: (looking suitably petrified) I can assure you that I will not eat from that tree. I won't even give it a second glance.

He: Now, listen, I don't think it is a good idea for you to remain alone. I believe it would be quite in perfect order if I created a helper for you. Would you like that?

Man: That would be very helpful, thank you.

That night, while Man, whom He had by now christened Adam, was asleep, He took a rib from his side, and closing the bone with some flesh, created a woman in the process.

Adam was ecstatic! A companion at last! And a very beautiful one for that matter!

He exultantly declared, "She will be called woman, for she was taken out of man."

At this time, Adam and Eve were both naked and were not bashful about that fact.

At this point in our poignant tale, a crafty and sinister old fellow insinuates himself into this idyllic setting. His name: The Serpent.

The Serpent engages Eve in dialogue:

The Serpent: Did He really say you must not eat from any of these trees?

Eve: Well, not quite. He merely warned us not to eat fruit from the tree in the middle of the garden nor even as much as touch it, lest we die.

The Serpent: (scoffing derisively) That's all baloney! You can't possibly die. Listen. He knows only too well that immediately you eat from that tree, you will become wise, like Him, and be able to discern good from evil.

Succumbing to relentless pressure from The Serpent, and in a bid to gratify a desire for rare and mysterious culinary delight and an understandable craving for illicit wisdom, she plucked a fruit from the tree and ate it. Being also a very generous woman and in the true spirit of matrimonial magnanimity and alliance, she gave Adam some to eat.

Immediately, they came into a conscious and bashful awareness of their nakedness and proceeded to cover themselves with fig leaves.

Wisdom had come to them!

Presently, He came into the garden on His daily stroll.

He: Adam, dear fellow, where art thou?

Adam: (from where he was hiding with Eve) I'm in hiding because I am naked.

He: Who told you that you were naked? Have you eaten from the tree?

Adam: (pointing at Eve) She gave me some fruit from the tree and I ate it.

He: (turning to Eve) What have you done?

Eve: (pointing at the serpent) He deceived me and I ate.

And God was very angry.

What happened in the garden of Eden? Adam and Eve allowed themselves to be lured into the false belief that they could somehow skip steps to gain divine wisdom and become like God. That singular false move of skipping steps is what is responsible for man's deviation from God's original plan of an existence of eternal paradise here on earth, and we are all still suffering the consequences to this day.

Yet another poignant example of skipping steps is presented in the story of Sarai and Abraham. Sarai, whom God later renamed Sarah, was the wife of Abraham. Hagar was the servant of Sarah. God had promised Abraham many descendants, but ten years after the promise, Sarah was still unable to have children, and they were both on the verge of becoming too old to have children at all. Sarah chose to give her servant Hagar to Abraham in accordance with the custom of that day so that Sarah could have a child through her. Hagar conceived and bore a child named Ishmael. Sarah later became jealous of her and despised her. Sarah began to deal harshly with her, and Hagar had to flee into the desert to escape the resentment of her mistress. The angel of the Lord met Hagar in the wilderness, commanding her to return to Abraham and Sarah. The angel relayed a promise from God: "I will surely multiply your offspring so that they cannot be numbered for multitude" as we can see in the scripture of Genesis chapter 16 and verse 10 (NIV).

Despite her despicable behavior toward Hagar, God later fulfilled His promise to Abraham and Sarah, and she gave birth to a son named Isaac. The lesson we learn, yet again, is that God's perfect love is unconditional. His love is not human love. Despite Sarah's attitude, in which she had attempted to skip the steps of showing love to Hagar and her son, God still fulfilled His promise to Abraham and Sarah in their old age. Also, we can see that God can and often does work through ways that appear unlikely from a human perspective. Abraham miraculously became a father at the age of eighty-six, and again at the age of ninety-nine. Isaac's mother, Sarah, was barren. God's promise to Abraham did not depend on human strength, and with God nothing is impossible. God used a seemingly impossible situation to make Abraham the father of the Jewish nation, just as He had promised. It is clear from this story that God works despite misguided human effort. One may even argue that Sarah had no business offering her servant to Abraham, and Abraham had no business sleeping with Hagar. And most certainly, Sarah was wrong to maltreat her servant as she did. Yet God worked through these situations. Hagar was blessed, and Abraham and Sarah were still the recipients of the promise. God's perfect love is incomparable, and His will is always accomplished regardless of human failing. Yes, regardless of how a situation looks from a human perspective, God continues to work both to accomplish His will and to fulfill His promises.

David was another person who skipped a step. He didn't go into battle with his men in a season in which he should have. What followed was a travesty. In a tale that would later show him up as an adulterer, schemer, murderer, and liar, David fell into the temptation of impregnating the wife of one of his officers at the war front. Attempting to take guilt off his neck, he made futile attempts to foist the pregnancy on the dutiful husband. When the attempts failed, he successfully arranged for the officer to be killed at the front line of battle. But David eventually repented, and God had mercy on him. He did not kill David. In fact, he went ahead to give David another son, Solomon, and allowed him to keep his throne. Once again, God's love was in operation.

Now, let us examine the contrary situation in which steps are not skipped and see how that relates to the working of God in our life. Skipping steps can mean the difference between life and death. Death, in this context, can be physical or it can be the death of a dream or a vision. Anytime you are faced with the dilemma of making a crucial decision, you are presented with two freedoms: a false one and a true one. False freedom is the freedom to do what you want. True freedom, on the other hand, is the freedom to do what you ought. However, just before you receive your answer, the enemy will send you counterfeit perspectives, doubts, unbelief, temptations, and tribulation. He will send you everything and anything he possibly can to get you to become faint in spirit and with chronic indecision. Remain steadfast.

Let us look at the turbulent story of Joseph in the scripture of Genesis chapter 37 (NIV). Joseph's odyssey presents a beautiful and eloquent example of what God's plan is for us when we refuse to skip steps and just place our total trust in Him. When we make up our mind to simply allow patience to complete its work, God will show up in marvelous ways. In all that Joseph went through, terrible and traumatic as they were, he could have skipped a step or two, but he remained steadfast and chose not to. Because of his dreams, in which he appeared to lord it over his siblings, his brothers became insanely jealous and plotted to kill him. Although he was saved by his brothers, Rueben and Judah, he was still sold into slavery to the Ishmaelites and taken to Egypt, where he eventually ended up working as a servant in Potiphar's house. He refused to succumb to the seductive efforts of Potiphar's wife, and although he ran away from his master's house, he was still accused of rape anyway. He was incarcerated in jail, where he was placed in charge of other prisoners. It just so happened that the king's chief cupbearer and his baker were also in jail. When they had dreams, Joseph successfully interpreted their dreams. In return, the cupbearer made a solemn promise to Joseph that he would remember his good deed. Two years passed, long after the cupbearer had left prison, Pharaoh had a dream. The cupbearer remembered the prisoner who had interpreted his own dream in prison. Pharaoh sent for Joseph. Joseph successfully interpreted the king's dream. In gratitude, Pharaoh made Joseph governor over all Egypt and his second-in-command. Famine was ravaging the land. Joseph's brothers came to Egypt to buy grain. They had to buy from Joseph, the governor of Egypt. Joseph was presented with critical choice-making. He had the freedom to do what he wanted or the freedom to do what he ought to do. Joseph made the right decision. He did what he felt he ought to do by his brothers. He chose to forgive his brothers.

Now, let us try to imagine what would have happened if Joseph had skipped any of those steps, or perhaps, just one step. Suppose he had given in to temptation and slept with Potiphar's wife? Do you for a moment imagine that events would have still culminated in the promotion of Joseph to the position of governor? When Joseph encountered his brothers, years after they had sold him into slavery, it was obvious that he had to wrestle with conflicting emotions. The emotion of love raged against his feeling of understandable anger. The urge to forgive juggled against the all-too-human disposition toward vengeance. But Joseph refused to skip a step. If you can somehow locate yourself in this message, the Lord wants me to encourage you. Even as some reader is holding this book in their hands, there are thoughts of skipping steps, switching one place for a more convenient one, dropping something for something deceptively better, or giving up prematurely, but God is saying, "Don't you do it!" The answer is right at your doorstep. Don't you make that false move! Just before the answer comes, you will experience mixed emotions, especially those of doubt. But you must refuse to skip a step. Let patience work it out in and for you. The blessing of the Lord makes right and adds no sorrow with it. You can be blessed and enjoy your blessing at the same time. Just wait on God. The answer is here. Just don't skip a step. To Him be all the glory. Amen.

CHAPTER 11

Purpose for Love

And now these three remain: faith, hope and
love. But the greatest of these is love.
> —1 Corinthians 13:13 (NIV)

The world is in a tragic state of traumatic flux. These are times of peril. These are times of selfishness. They are times of the self-aggrandizement that celebrates the ego to the high heavens while relegating love to the obscure background. Sadly, the consequence of all these is that love appears to be fast becoming an outdated and an antiquated concept whose very understanding has also become quite bewildering to most people. Is this so surprising? Not really. Our world is in turmoil. We are all great civil engineers. The only tragedy in this fact is that we continually employ our engineering skills to erect walls of discord, disharmony, and disenchantment between ourselves. Terrorism is on a daily high alert globally. Anywhere you turn, people are living lives of trepidation and quiet desperation. Many people do not know whether they stand the slightest chance of avoiding deportation to their homeland even after living in the United States all of their lives. Many are afraid of stepping out of their homes for fear of being killed by a stray bullet. A host of others live in daily paranoia that every person they meet has a hidden agenda of some sort and wants something from them. The list of horrendous possibilities is seemingly endless.

Where does it all stop? Where is the hope for mankind? Only love can put a halt to the global tragedy. The only hope for mankind is love. What the world needs is love. We must all commit to building bridges of love between one another's hearts. That is why love is the greatest challenge for humanity as a whole. We each have an individual mission. We all have a collective mission. That mission is to continue to spread this love. Indeed, the world, now more than ever, needs to feel and see love. I know that is a tall order. However, like the old adage says, "The journey of a thousand miles begins with the first step." Indeed, even a trip of a single mile will have to begin with the first step. The great thing about love is that it is infectious. Love is contagious. Love still works. If each person decides to give love rather than hate, we could find ourselves collectively changing this world, even if it is only within our own little microcosm. On the individual level, we are so busy fighting each other while on the corporate level of nationhood, we are no less preoccupied with exerting competing forces for control and power. In all these, we have lost our fight for love.

Yes, I believe we have to fight for love. We have to fight for love in our marriages. We have to fight for love in our schools and in our churches. Indeed, we must see the quest for love as a serious battle. True love is something that we must work at in an active manner for it to really manifest itself in our lives and that of others. True love goes beyond an ordinary feeling to become a "doing." Most people assume that love is merely and only a "feel good" emotion. This is an easy trap to fall into because that thinking is wrong. Love is actually a very active verb that manifests itself more in the "doing" than in the "feeling." There is nothing worthwhile in life that does not demand hard work. Love is not an exception. We must work at it. This hard work involves two things. The first is controlling the basic human nature in us. The second is developing the attitudes that allow us to fight "unlovable actions." This is because, ultimately, love is all that matters.

This millennial generation knows little or nothing about the brand of love that the baby boomers grew up on. We grew up with songs that talked about love and not lust. Examples of such great songs remain evergreen in our memories. Thankfully, they are there in the archives for us to listen to anytime we wish. They include:

"Always & Forever" by Luther Vandross; "With These Hands" by The Temptations; "Ain't No Mountain High Enough" by Marvin Gaye and Tammi Terrell, and so many more of such great love songs. The lyrics of some of today's songs make me want to run and hide my face somewhere in utter shame! And it is not because I am that old either. It is simply because, apart from being nothing short of embarrassingly graphic and totally disrespectful, they leave nothing to the imagination. The very real fear is that if one is exposed to such lyrics for too long, one becomes "inoculated with the virus of lust," so to speak, and having become immune to the graphic messages, one can no longer see or hear anything wrong with such songs. The rather disturbing contemporary trend is that it is in perfect order to call out the name of your children's mother and liken her to a female dog and hurt and ridicule her just because she wouldn't do something you insisted upon. It is also apparently quite normal to have a woman on the side because your wife doesn't believe in oral sex. The abominable list goes on.

Admittedly, we did have a few songs that encouraged unfaithful love, but their central theme was still love. "Me & Mrs. Jones" by Billy Paul is one example of such songs. It might have been as misplaced as a nine-dollar bill, but at least it didn't say, "Kill Mr. Jones," as some would brazenly put it today.

We grew up in an era when, if a neighbor fell ill, we would check up on him or her and visit with a pot of soup. These days, we go into our houses, lock our doors, draw our blinds, and simply mind our own business. We celebrate this selfish tendency as a welcome sign of the times. Where has love for our neighbors and for our neighborhood gone? We would visit our ailing elders. Today, we send them text messages, and whether they know how to use the text feature on their phone or they don't is no concern of ours. Well, they had better own a cell phone in the first place!

Love is still powerful. There is no greater power, in heaven or on earth, than pure unconditional love. This should hardly come as a surprise. In its highest nature, love is the force we recognize as the will of God. Love is the highest and the most luminous state anyone can possibly hope to achieve. It makes the difference between the life and the death of relationships. People don't speak in civil tones to one another anymore. Disrespect has become an accepted norm of our society. Disrespect blocks the channel of love. Love is a totally reciprocal entity, if only because it must be given in order to be received. This, in itself, reveals the paradox that love is because the very concept means that someone has to initiate it while also meaning everyone has an obligation to initiate it! Yes, love is not your simple dimple in the cheek phenomenon. Rather, love is the totality of the physics of life. Love is never just a simple occurrence for love always requires something of you. Love must cost you something. We need to know the cost of love and pay the price. Love is the greatest and the most luminous entity on earth, and like anything of immense value, it must have a price tag. The walk of love simply cannot be an easy enterprise to embark upon.

We need to learn to display our love by meeting the needs of others. We need to meet their practical needs and their spiritual needs for what is generosity if not merely love in action? Our love should be seen through edification and encouragement. Our love should be seen through patience and kindness. Our love should be seen through courtesy and humility. Our love should be seen through good temper and gentleness. Our love should be seen through unselfishness and sincerity.

The easiest and the most common denominator in our lives is the propensity to find something wrong in any and everyone. What is the panacea for this classic dilemma?

It is simple. Paul, in the scripture in his First Letter to Peter, in chapter 4, verse 8 (NIV), said, "Above all things; have intense and unfailing love for one another; for love covers a multitude of sins." Indeed, it is only through our love that we can cover the multitude of sins of others.

It is our perspective that confuses the entire matter of love, making it difficult for us to be givers. Perhaps this is the reason why people hold back their love. Should I be so selfish as to reserve my love for only those who meet my own special desires and needs? Is love supposed to be discriminatory? Isn't love supposed to be sacrificial? Is love supposed to be biased or prejudiced? Could that be the source of racism? Is it because people just don't know how to love? Is it because love requires something from your essence, and you believe that somehow it ends up diminishing you, instead of enhancing you? Do you, for instance, subscribe to the saying that money doesn't change who you are, but rather enhances who you are? If you believe in this premise concerning monetary gain, you will have to accord love the same privilege. Because in truth, love does not change who you are. It merely enhances the best of who you are. When you decide to love, instead of indulging in hatred, jealousy, or selfishness, you increase your essence and become bigger than who you are.

When you give it serious thought, isn't this what life is all about? God allowed us to be in this world so as to grow and be bigger than what we were at our last birthday. Shouldn't we be on the path of continuous growth? If that be the case, by what standard or measurement, or better still, in what dimension are we growing?

We are never standing still in life. We are in a state of constant motion. We are moving in some direction or the other. We are either becoming more loving or growing colder. I am, by no means, throwing stones at anyone, and you will appreciate why I am not unduly castigating if you remember the contents of my introduction to this book. I will be the first to admit that life has its own peculiar way of making the heart grow cold. Pain and suffering can touch you in so many different ways, even when you are not at the receiving end, and especially when you can see the pain and suffering of the people around you and all across the world. Such human agony speaks to an individual's heart in different ways, and quite often, it can make one doubt the very existence of God. We now have a dilemma in accurately situating God in the affairs of man. For if there is no God, then love really doesn't exist. On the other hand, if there is a God, then where is He, especially in the light of all the evil that appears to be pervading the land?

Author Robert Jeffress, in his book *How Can I Know?* addresses this notion of God's presence in the world. He puts matters in a nutshell by suggesting that humanity is largely confused by the evil that is seen and then by a God that is not seen. As Jeffress points out in his book, "God has given human beings the freedom to obey or disobey His divine decrees. While theologians will continue to argue the extent of that freedom, the bottom line is that God does not coerce anyone to obey Him." Apologist Norman Geisler, on his own part, writes, "Since God is love, he cannot force himself on anyone against his will. Forced love is not love; it is rape. And God is not a divine rapist. Where freedom exists, there will always be the possibility of evil."

Robert Jeffress, in the same book, reports that Author Phillip Yancey's father was a devout Christian and a gifted Bible teacher. Yet in the twilight years of his life, he suffered from a debilitating nerve disease that left him permanently confined to a bed. He watched his adult daughter suffer the effects of a severe form of diabetes. He experienced crushing financial pressure. At the height of his personal crisis, he sent a letter to his family members, confessing that he was starting to question many of the things he once believed and taught others. However, there remained three truths about which Yancey proclaimed his total conviction:

> Life is difficult.
> God is merciful.
> Heaven is for sure.

Ultimately, God gave us a free will. He gave us the power to choose our direction in life although being well aware of our decisions even before we make them, or even before we were formed in our mother's womb. He is not to blame for the craziness in our world, neither is he to blame for the spiritual complacency of humanity. God is actively at work in our lives when and if we give him permission to be so active. When we accept Jesus as Lord of our life, then we give Him permission to take control at the helm of the ship. He is responsible for our lives, but He still doesn't block us from every wrong decision we insist on making. Quite often, we learn more by what we do wrong than what we do right. However, He is there to keep us from utterly destroying ourselves. He becomes our protector and advisor and gives us the purpose for love. He gives us the strength to keep fighting for love. The world needs love. Therefore, the world needs you. You are love for God created you in His perfect image. In you is the power of love and to love and to be loved. The only tragedy is that we have twisted the concept of love so that we now have those who can give love but do not understand how to receive love.

Many persons are abused by loved ones and remain in these unhealthy relationships out of fear. They don't understand that love is what love does. Hurting you, smacking you, cursing you, and being the personification of evil toward you with words and deeds are not in the spirit of God's love. Love is kind but does not demand perfection from you. Love is patient but does not ask you to be bottomlessly tolerant. Love keeps no record of wrongs but does not seek to confer incessant stupidity on you. God is pure, and when you are in the presence of love, it makes you feel secure and good about yourself, even when it corrects you. You know love is making you bigger and taller and helping to straighten out your back, to lift your shoulders and your head above your circumstances. Love is working on making you a better person, so as to make you understand yourself better and to fully accept who God has created you to be. Love is there to gently guide you yet demand change from you so that you can go in the right direction. Love is for others. The purpose God created you is to love. God's purpose for love is to give. Your purpose for being here is to give love to a dying and sick world wherever you can and whenever you can. The purpose of love is to change where you live.

In this particular vein, I am specifically speaking to those women who have confused love with institutionalized slavery. You are not a punching bag nor are you a doormat. God does not require you to stay in a relationship where you are consistently disrespected and hurt, both physically and emotionally. We will have our downtimes in our marriages, but this should be the exception and not the norm. Let me make this crystal clear. I am not advocating divorce. I merely advocate safety. If you do not feel safe, or are not safe, then know that love is not involved. Love does not behave itself unseemly, neither does it rejoice in your demise.

The story about the woman caught in adultery comes to my mind. The scribes and the Pharisees had dragged the woman before

Jesus and reminded Him that according to the Law of Moses, the woman should be stoned to death. Jesus, in the scripture in John chapter 8, verse 7 (NIV), said to them, "Let him who is without sin among you be the first to cast the first stone." After they had left Him with the woman, He told her that since there was no one around to condemn her, He wouldn't condemn her either and asked her to "go and sin no more." I once heard Pastor John Hagee preach on this story. He put the entire story in a new light for me. Pastor Hagee's summary was that to forgive without demanding a change in conduct is to make the grace of God an accomplice to evil. Jesus asked the woman to go but to sin no more. Forgiveness is a divine command. How many times should I forgive? Seventy times seven is the answer. The word of God tells us that if you don't forgive others, then He won't forgive you. Jesus forgave the woman but also said, "Go and sin no more." He demanded a change in her behavior. He demanded a change in her direction. So forgiveness is to be given, but a change in behavior is expected. If not, could you, perhaps, be promoting the grace of God as an accomplice to evil? Seek help and counseling in your abusive relationship. Do what you need to do so as to have a clear mind, but do not sit and let the very life get sucked out of you. Be courageous. Fight for love. Fight for true love.

Yes, you can and should fight for true love. Yet the fight for true love cannot come without tremendous personal sacrifice. Each time we choose to love another, it will cost us something. It will cost us time. It will cost us effort. It may even cost us money. For nothing ennobling comes without the sacrifice that borders on the divine. And that is why we are told to count the cost before making the commitment. Developing the walk of love is like digging for gold. To gain access to gold, we must mine for it. We must scrape through endless layers of earthy crust to gain access to the emeralds contained in the bowels of the earth. True love is rarely found on the surface of life, and we must eagerly pursue and seek it in the subterranean depths of the human condition. To Him be all the glory. Amen.

CHAPTER 12

Nurturing Love Through Relationships

Love your neighbor as yourself. There is no commandment greater than this.
—Mark 12:31 (NIV)

Many Christians hurt. The experience in many ministries is that the greater majority of such hurt result from broken relationships. I have a women's ministry called Gracious Women's Fellowship. It is a venue for hurting women. I hold a breakfast meeting or fellowship once a month in which I bring the Word of God to the participants. Afterward, I do a healing and deliverance session to break the bonds off these women. God has blessed this ministry tremendously, and I have seen women set free from abusive relationships or from a certain spiritual place where they have been stuck to starting their own businesses and ministries. They are running with the vision. In this ministry, I take particular care and pains to teach submission and humility but also strive to balance that with the scriptures that say, "Jesus came that you might have life and have it more abundantly" (John 10:10, NIV), and "I wish, above all things, that you prosper, be in health even as your soul prospers" (3 John 1:2, NIV). The reason why I lay some emphasis on these teachings is because for the women to attain their complete healing, they must also learn to play their part as Christians before love can be nurtured in their new and future relationships.

I believe that in covering us with His banner of love, God wants His people healed and made whole. I believe my part in the vineyard is to help people get there, not just women, but all men. I believe my life's lessons are contained in something the Lord said to me many years ago. He said, "I am making you magnanimous." Well, I thought that meant great! Awesome! Hallelujah! However, something in my spirit said, "You'd better look that word up because it may not mean what you think it means." What I learned was that, very soon, I would have to suffer for the Gospel's sake, and that forgiveness would be my way out. I have suffered challenges with my health, I have suffered challenges in both my health and personal relationships. However, my healing, not only physical, but also spiritual, has seen me through while the greater part of that healing has come through a better understanding of the place of relationships in my own life as a Christian.

The Bible is a book of relationships. It shows us what our relationship with God is meant to be and how we can have that kind of relationship. In teaching us the same thing in our relationship with others, it shows us how we should interact with and treat our fellow Christians. It also shows us how we are to view those who do not believe. Because it is the physical world around us that we can see and touch, many times that physical world seems more real than the spiritual world in which we connect and communicate with God. This means that sometimes we let our earthly relationships become more important than our relationship with God. This should not be so, and therein lies the critical need for us to not only nurture love through our relationships, but to also strike the spiritual balance between our love walk with God and our love for our brothers.

But first we must recognize that God provides us with the tools with which to come into a perfect understanding of His message of love to us. For me, such a tool came in the form of award-winning sportswriter Mitch Albom's book *Tuesdays with Morrie: An Old Man, a Young Man, and Life's Greatest Lesson.* Two decades ago, the author had been a student of sociology professor Morris Schwartz at Brandeis University. Mitch Albom recounts how, as his old professor and mentor was dying, he renewed their warm relationship. The dying man seemed to have developed a life-affirming attitude toward his terminal illness. Albom committed to weekly Tuesday visits to his teacher and interpreted their encounter as his last "class" and the book that resulted from it as a "term paper" with the subject: The Meaning of Life. Albom presents his professor's unassailable aphorisms, like, "Love is the only rational act. Love each other or perish." Additionally, Albom learned that "death ends a life, not a relationship." Albom also talked about forgiveness in his book. The book ultimately reminded me of what God was really saying about the life I would live in Him. Some twenty-six years later, I can say that I am learning to live the courage of my convictions, as Morrie did.

I walked with Morrie and Mitch through every Tuesday experience, not realizing until the end of the book that I had actually joined their journey by assimilating myself into their experience. I was shocked to find myself crying at the end of the story, and that was when I realized just how much I had assimilated the book and the extent of my emotional engagement with it. Initially, I didn't feel it, nor did I see it, but Morrie and Mitch's journey had uncannily joined up with my own spiritual journey in discovering the hidden places in my life. I ended up asking myself some questions. For instance: "Why am I doing what I'm doing?" I spend so much time at work, or thinking about work, and now I spend so much time on schooling although thank God, it is spiritually based. This sort of reflection is allowing me to consider the possibility that I might just be getting my priorities mixed up. Do I devote enough time to my family? The answer is no. It certainly is not like I used to. Do I devote sufficient time to building my relationship with the Lord? The answer is no. It is definitely not like I used to. Is my ministry thriving? The answer is no. It is not like it used to.

In that case, what in my life seems to have assumed greater importance than my family and ministry? It is work. Mitch came to this realization at the beginning of Morrie's suffering. That was why he flew every Tuesday from where he was to be with Morrie. Those visits with Morrie became his most treasured classroom, he would learn more about himself than he ever possibly could in any leadership course. Mitch learned courage through Morrie's own courage in his determination to not die while still living. Morrie gave Mitch the best gift a person could ever give a person. He gave Mitch an opportunity to reflect on his life even before the possibility of finding himself in a similar situation of facing death. In ministering to Mitch in this manner, he also gave all of us that same gift. While we may have many responsibilities as leaders in our churches and our organizations, there is nothing more important than relationships. No matter a church organization's ecumenical philosophy in the dissemination of the Word of God and the teaching of religious principles, what is of paramount importance is for it to promote the nurturing of love through relationships. This is Morrie's message to all of us. This is where the battle lies for me. I now valued the people God has put in my life; and when I can't spend quality time with my mother and other loved ones or when I neglect to send a card in a timely fashion to a grieving friend or just fail to pick up the phone to say hello, I feel like all the other things I do in life are not only ineffectual, but may even be nullified. We never know where life's twists and turns will take us. It's imperative for us to do what we can, and while we can, to show our family and friends how much we care. That ought to be the watchword of a true believer. I am convinced that it's only what I do for Christ that will last. That is the essence of my spiritual journey.

So what does the Word of God say about relationships? First, we are told to love the Lord first. In the scripture in Mark chapter 12, verse 30 (NIV), Jesus tells us that our first responsibility is to Him. "And you shall love the Lord your God with all your heart and with all your soul and with all your mind and with all your strength." This same theme is repeated in the scripture in Matthew chapter 22, verse 37 (NIV): "Jesus replied: 'Love the Lord your God with all your heart and with all your soul and with all your mind.'" Putting the Lord first in our lives is the most important decision we could ever make. A life built around anything else but God is merely a life built on shifting sand. Too many people today wonder why their lives are filled with so much misery. The reason is that these people refuse to submit to God and live for Him. Many of us build our lives on fantasy and deception. It is because our foundation was untrustworthy in the first place. We place our faith in man rather than God, and then when man lets us down, we wonder why our life has fallen to pieces. There is no firmer foundation for life than a relationship with God through faith in Jesus Christ. It is this relationship that must be first and foremost in the life of man. In other words, only when Jesus is our priority can we be assured that our other relationships are based on a firm foundation.

Secondly, we are told to love our neighbor. This command was repeated many times throughout the Bible. But let us look at the scripture in Mark chapter 12, verse 31 (NIV). It says, "Love your neighbor as yourself. There is no commandment greater than this."

Loving God and loving others as much as we love ourselves is obviously a very important matter. It is also very important to get the order correct. God first, and everything else follows. This becomes even more crucial in the relationship between husband and wife. The book of Genesis tells us that at creation, God instituted the union of marriage. When Jesus was questioned about marriage, He reiterated the words in Genesis but added some words that make the marriage union even more important. He answered, "Have you not read that He who created them from the beginning made them male and female, and said, 'Therefore a man shall leave his father and his mother and hold fast to his wife, and the two shall become one flesh?' So they are no longer two but one flesh. What therefore God has joined together, let not man separate." It is clear that God designed marriage to be between one man and one woman "for as long as they both shall live." This means the marriage bond was designed by God to be permanent, and it is the failure of humanity to take this union more seriously that has resulted in much of the moral decay we see in our world today.

The third premise is our relationship with other believers. When a person becomes a believer in Jesus Christ, that person also begins a new relationship with others who have done the same. As would be expected, the new believer becomes a member of the family of believers, and they build each other up in the faith. Their bond is really quite special because it is the Holy Spirit living within that empowers them to have a special relationship with one another. In John chapter 13, verses 34 and 35 (NIV), Jesus says, "A new commandment I give to you, that you love one another: just as I have loved you, you also are to love one another. By this all people will know that you are my disciples, if you have love for one another." A relationship with God results in a believer having a special connection with other believers, and this is because the love of God binds them together in a way nothing else can. As Christians, we are supposed to encourage one another, and that is why the scripture in Romans chapter 15, verse 2 (NIV) says, "Let each of us please his neighbor for his good, to build him up." Believers are all part of the body of Christ, and as one body, we are to support one another. We should help those brothers and sisters in need and not merely be concerned for our own needs. We should also be quick to forgive a fellow believer when they offend us. These all constitute the true essence of nurturing love in our relationships. Ultimately, the true test of the effectiveness of our love for one another is that nonbelievers should see something different and wonderful about the way Christians treat each other.

Finally, our assignment also rests on the platform of evangelism. After Jesus's resurrection, before He ascended to heaven, He commanded His disciples to go and make disciples of all nations, baptizing them in the name of the Father and of the Son and of the Holy Spirit and teaching them to observe all that He had commanded them, assuring them that He ever remained with them and to the end of time. This command applies to us as His disciples also. Jesus does not want anyone to suffer eternal punishment. He came to earth, died on the cross, and has entrusted to us the task of taking His message to the people of the world. Our ultimate mission is to bring light to a world darkened by sin, showing people the way to the Savior.

Although Jesus stressed how important it is that we put Him first in our lives when He said in Matthew 10:37 (NIV), "Whoever loves father or mother more than me is not worthy of me, and whoever loves son or daughter more than me is not worthy of me," He did not say that we are not to love others. He only meant that we must love Him more than all others. There are so many different types of relationships that we should nurture, such as with parents, children, friends, and members of the extended family. However, the quality of all these relationships will hinge on the quality of our relationship with God. When our relationship with God is our most important relationship, all other relationships will be what they are meant to be.

Some of my closest relationships in life were with my own parents. My father passed on July 9, 1998, and my mother passed on November 1, 2015. Needless to say, the transition of each of my parents to their heavenly home brought a major change to my life. My mother was the rock of my life. She was my cheerleader and the source of my wisdom. There wasn't anything I attempted in life in which my mother did not cheer me on, telling me, "You can do it!" Although her transition has left a void in my life, it has also caused me to see my Savior in a new light. This was a major transition and turn in my spiritual journey. I was sure that I had a good relationship with God, and that I had a genuine inclination for His pulse. But after my mother passed, I became assailed with unbelief and doubt. I believe that I had expected the Lord to set up my mother's death in a time and manner that would meet my own purpose and convenience, such that I would be there to hold her hand. But as it turned out, my mother died suddenly. There was no real sickness as such. She did not have cancer. There was no warning of her passing. There were no yellow or flashing lights. We had taken her to the hospital one Saturday morning because she was feeling faint. The doctor diagnosed her with a bladder infection for which she received treatment. My husband and I left her at 11:00 p.m., only to receive a phone call from the doctor at 6:00 a.m., asking if I wanted the hospital to revive my mother. I cannot explain the shock that overwhelmed me in that instant, but I arrived at the hospital thirty minutes to meet the horrific news that my mother was gone. It happened just like that. There was no explanation. At my daughters' insistence, I had an autopsy done. The result came back as "Death by natural causes."

The first test and struggle was to accept God's will. I had experienced the death of many loved ones before this, including my dear father. But my mother's sudden passing made the reality of death starkly clear and magnified. There is no coming back. Death is final in this state.

God reminded me through the passing of my mother that He cannot be placed in a box, and neither can He be pinholed and controlled. Although God will make us feel we are the only person in His heart and mind, He also always reminds us that this is not so. He loves because he is love. His unconditional love is not based on any virtue we may think we possess. God is no respect of person. None of us has a monopoly of God or His love. He truly loves unconditionally. Finally, I was learning on this new spiritual journey that the only place for me to go was to the place of "trust." Once I started accepting my new place in God, the place of "trust," I could see how better off my mother and father were. I could see that my mother had become free of the bondages, tentacles, and burdens of this world. I could see that my mother was now with more of real and celestial family than whatever family she had left on earth. I could see that my mother was happy with her Savior and was finally at peace. Ultimately, I could see that God has a bigger purpose for my life. What about you?

CHAPTER 13

Love Wants You Back

We had to celebrate and be glad, because this brother of yours was dead and is alive again; he was lost and is found.

—Luke 15:32 (NIV)

To different degrees, we all seem to have a measure of the "call to the wild" in us. It is that part of us that seeks to explore areas we've never before explored. It is a bent, or propensity, if you will, to "color outside of the lines" or to get out of a world that has apparently boxed us in, if not permanently, at least for a while. Given the proclivity of the human spirit for expedition, that may well be tolerable as long as the exploration itself does not take us into irredeemable territory. Yes, I can plainly hear you say, "Sometimes, there may be no indications or warning signs that one is exploring in a danger zone, and one may not know until one gets there." That is true. In the book of Luke, in chapter 15 (NIV), Luke tells us about the prodigal son who demanded his own share of inheritance while his father was still alive. He had decided not to wait until his father's death to come into his estate. Why did the young man make such a demand, one might ask? I believe he was responding to a "call to the wild." The prodigal son had lived under his father's roof, and to the best of his ability, had made himself amenable to his father's rules. It would seem that there does come a time when rules become too rigid for us. There comes a time when we believe our situation calls for a little bending of the rules. The problem with that is you simply don't know the various probabilities and consequences that could manifest as a result of breaking the rules. After all, rules are created for a reason. Rules are made to ensure orderliness and to preserve us. Some of the reasons for the creation of rules are for our safety and protection. Therein lies the mystery of exploration, making exploration all the more intriguing.

So the prodigal son, having been protected from the wiles of the world, now decided he wanted to see what the other side of the world was like. He would experience both fortunate and unfortunate results of his adventure. He answered the "call to the wild" and headed out on his exploration. Eventually, he found himself in wrong company, having been caught up with the wrong people, and immersing himself in their culture, ended up breaking every rule he had previously held dear in his sheltered upbringing. He had strayed away from his father's protection and guidance, only to find himself in what could be likened to a pigpen. Now, the pigpen can have as many connotations as your imagination can come up with, but I think I will leave you to fill in your own blank spaces.

Exploration has the potential to take all kinds of twists and turns, and it can cause you to swerve out of control. Bishop Keith Reed Sr. of Sharon Baptist Church in Philadelphia, preaches often using a familiar cliché: "You went too far and stayed too long!" This clearly validates my point here. Exploration can very quickly dissolve into a serious problem. Indeed, although you started out in full control at the helm, you neither knew, nor could you possibly see, what was up ahead. While you may not necessarily be faulted for wanting to explore all life has to offer, you still have to remain in conscious reality of the fact that you may end up losing control of the exploration and ultimately find yourself a ship floundering in the open ocean without a sail.

I know only too well that there is someone reading this right now who can attest to the dangers of exploration. You got caught up and found yourself in the pigpen. As a result, you may have lost your job security, ended up divorced, acquired HIV, got voted out of your church, saw your son become an opioid addict, and perhaps became a food addict yourself. The list of possibilities is endless.

The Bible tells us that Jesus was tempted at all points, just as we are yet without sin. He, too, suffered betrayal, rejection, and disappointment, and all this was substantiated when He went to the garden of Gethsemane and pleaded with God to "let this cup pass from me." He didn't want to suffer the cross, and although he was God, He still wanted God to break the rules or at least bend them a little on His behalf. However, even in His anguish, Jesus still recognized that God's way was the best way, and He finally said, "Not my will Lord, but thine will be done." Love's greater purpose prevailed, as breaking the rule would have derailed God's entire plan for our destiny. Jesus came that we might have life and have it more abundantly. His purpose is for us to enjoy the life and the world he has given us, but we have to let him stay at the helm of our ship.

At the end of the day, we must fall back on the old adage that says, "Freedom is not doing what I want but doing what I aught." This saying is hard to follow; who can receive it? Love, true love, requires genuine sacrifice. The scripture in 1 Corinthians chapter 6, verse 12, says, "All things are lawful, but all things are not expedient unto you." That is the King James version of the Bible. The version in the New International says, "'I have the right to do anything,' you say, but not everything is beneficial." Many people discover this truth not too long after answering the "call to the wild." For some others, they would have gone almost too far for redemption before reality hits them. Yet no matter how far gone you are, Jesus is waiting to receive you with open arms.

Let us recall the fate that befell the prodigal son in the book of Luke. As the parable goes, when he came to his senses, he said to himself, "How many of my father's hired servants have food to spare, and here I am starving to death. I will set out and go back to my father and say to him: Father, I have sinned against heaven and against you. I am no longer worthy to be called your son; make me like one of your hired servants, so he got up and went to his father." Even while he was still a long way off, his father spotted him approaching and having pity for his son, ran to embrace him and welcome him with open arms. Not only that; he threw a big party to welcome him home. We are told that this gesture did not go down well with his other son, who felt that the prodigal one did not deserve such a welcome after squandering his father's wealth on a life of easy virtue. But the father replied, "We had to celebrate and be glad, because this brother of yours was dead and is alive again; he was lost and is found."

The end of your own story will be like that of the prodigal son. You may have "gone too far and stayed too long," but love wants you back. The fortunate thing for you, the prodigal son or daughter, is that God's arms are always wide open, beckoning to you to come back home. He never closes his arms, no matter how far left you may have gone. You are the sweat on his brow in that garden of Gethsemane. The humanity in him did not want to suffer, but the divinity in him was willing to go all the way for you. Among those great balls of sweat that Jesus lost was one that was solely for you. He remembered His love for you, and He refused to give in to the flesh. He cried, "Let your will be done, Father!" That is how you should cry out today to your Savior, Jesus Christ: "I can't do it by myself. I can't handle this world without You. I am tired of living in the pigpen. Come and save me, Jesus. I am the sweat of Your brow. I surrender to Your great love. I understand Your love is unconditional. There is nothing that I have done that shocks You or would separate me from Your love forever. Forgive me."

The beauty of it all is that God has always wanted you back, and He will stop at nothing to show you His great love. Your journey of exploration is not wasted. God will use every part of it to teach you His precepts and to show you how to comfort someone else who went astray. God will use you in ways you can't even begin to imagine because your value has just gone up. You are learning how to abound and be abased. You are learning that God's way is always better because He Knows the beginning from the end and everything in between. You are learning that your vision is myopic. You really can't figure out any situation because there are just too many unknown variables you can't see or control. God will use you in marvelous ways. All you have to do is say, "I give up. I give up the wild and surrender to our Lord's liquid love." To Him be all the glory. Amen.

CHAPTER 14

Supernatural Love

Love bears all things, believes all things, hopes all things, endures all things.
— 1 Corinthians 13:7 (NIV)

The love of man is natural and is therefore necessarily limited, both in expression and in scope. The love of God, on the other hand, is supernatural and being totally divine, can only be shared by the spirit of the Lord. But then, this is not surprising for "God, Himself, is love." Our immediate challenge may be how to define the very concept of God as love.

The *American Heritage Dictionary* defines love, meaning "human love," as "an intense affection for another person based on familial or personal ties." Almost invariably, this "intense affection" is as a result of a sexual attraction for that other person. We tend to proclaim our love for other people when we are attracted to them and when they make us feel good. That explains why a key phrase in that dictionary definition of love is "based on." This phrase implies that as humans, we tend to love conditionally. Put differently, we love someone because they have fulfilled a condition that allows us to love them. That is why we also say things like, "I love you because you are beautiful" or "I love you because of your warmth toward me," or "I love you because you are such a fun person to be with."

Not only is human love conditional; it is also mercurial in nature. To be mercurial is to be subject to sudden or unpredictable changes of mood or mind. Love that is based on feelings and emotions that can change from one moment to the next. A common ground for divorce these days is the oft-quoted refrain, "I no longer love my husband" or "I am no longer in love with her." It seems all it takes is for there to be a rough patch in a marriage, and a couple declare that they no longer "feel" love for each other and are ready to call it quits. Evidently, the marriage vow of "till death do us part" appears to have assumed the interpretation that a couple can part at the "death" of their love rather than at their physical death!

That is where the love of God differs. It is unconditional. Unconditional love is difficult to comprehend. Frankly, it seems the love that parents have for their children is as close to unconditional love as we can get without the help of God's love in our lives. Generally, parents continue to love their children through good times and bad times, and they don't stop loving them if they don't meet up to expectations. We make a choice to love our children even when we consider them unlovable. Our love doesn't stop when we don't "feel" love for them. This is the easiest way to appreciate God's unconditional love for us. Even then, God's love still transcends the human definition of love to a point that is hard for us to comprehend.

The sphere in which we are supposed to practice what is akin to God's unconditional love the most is marriage. Because the marriage covenant can be compared to God's new covenant through our Lord Jesus Christ, a covenant marriage is intended by God to be a lifelong relationship that exemplifies unconditional love and total mutual reconciliation. That is why, very much like the supernatural love of God, the love in a marriage is not supposed to be your ordinary kind of love. Rather, it's supposed to be your "in spite of love." A covenant is an eternal commitment with and to God. A couple's marriage vow is a vow to God, and to each other, to remain steadfast to each other while purposefully growing in their covenant relationship with God. Did you know that although the two words "contract" and "covenant" seem so similar, they are actually very different? You can negotiate your way out of a contract, but you cannot negotiate your way out of a covenant. This should hardly come as a surprise. The very soul of covenant marriage is "the steadfast love of God," which comes from the very heart of God and never ceases.

The stark reality of marriage is that the initial euphoric romantic glow, in which couples expect to have their emotional needs met, very soon dissipates in the face of the practical realities of their joint existence as husband and wife. For some, gratification of these emotional needs has become an addiction, and they become unhappy whenever they are denied it. But as Bishop T. D. Jakes said, "This is dependency, not love. It is shallow, not deep. It is a mere feeling, not a commitment…a feeling that can change as moods or circumstances change… and if the feeling vanishes, even temporarily, then it is easy to decide that love has ended." The mature love that is needed to sustain marriage has a spiritual component that converts you from a self-oriented person to a spouse-oriented person, in such a way that your spouse's welfare and happiness becomes greater than yours. After all, covenant love is actually the most accurate estimate of just how much we supply another's needs. That is also why the real love of a marriage is what results after years of surmounting difficulties together. The word love is a very active verb. This means that love is not just a pleasant feeling. Rather, it is a way of regarding someone on a long-term basis.

The late Bishop Norman Vincent Peale, author of the all-time classic *The Power of Positive Thinking*, once had to counsel a distraught young lady named Mary.

Mary: I don't love my husband anymore.
Peale: How do you know that?
Mary: I don't feel loving toward him any longer, that's why. I feel nothing.
Peale: Love is more than a feeling. Simply commit, for the next one month, to acting as though you love him, whether you think you do or not. Do this, regardless of how you feel or don't feel. The important thing is how you act, not how you feel. To act this way is not deception. It is the practical dramatization of a hoped-for image of what is to come. This is unconditional love. The really true love.

Mary's marriage was salvaged.

The Bible tells us that "God is love" in 1 John 4:8 (NIV). But how can we even begin to comprehend that truth? There are many scriptures that offer us God's definition of love. The most well-known verse is in John chapter 3, verse 16 (NIV): "For God so loved the world, that he gave his only begotten Son, that whosoever believeth in him should not perish, but have everlasting life." So one way God defines love is in the act of giving. However, what God gave us was not a mere gift-wrapped present. God sacrificed His only Son so that we, who put our faith in His Son, will not spend eternity separated from Him. This is an amazing type of love, is it not? After all, we are the ones who choose to reject God, yet it is God who is being magnanimous enough to heal the fracture through His intense personal sacrifice. All we have to do is accept His gift.

Another scripture about God's love is in Romans chapter 5, verse 8 (NIV): "But God commendeth his love toward us, in that, while we were yet sinners, Christ died for us." In this verse, there are no conditions placed on God's love for us. God doesn't say, "As soon as you stop sinning, I will love you" nor does He say, "I will only sacrifice my Son if you promise to love Me." In fact, this particular scripture makes it clear that God's love is unconditional since He sent His Son to die for us while we were still unlovable sinners! Can you beat that? We didn't have to make any promises to God before we could experience His love. His love for us has always been there, and because of that, He did all the giving and sacrificing long before we were even aware that we needed His love. God is love, and His love is very different from human love. His love is unconditional, and not being mercurial, is not based on feelings or emotions. He doesn't love us because we're lovable or because we make Him feel good. He loves us because He is love. He created us to have a loving relationship with Him, and He sacrificed His own Son to restore that relationship.

Indeed, God's love is perfectly sacrificial. Jesus Christ, God in human flesh, endured the pain of the cross because He loves us. Jesus gave up His place with God in heaven in order to come down to earth, experience humility, shame, suffering, and death so that anyone who trusts in Him will be forgiven their sins and can enjoy the close personal relationship with Him for which they were created. He did this willingly and purely out of the motivation of love. Worldly love, in contrast, is selfish, self-serving, and cares more for what it gets from a relationship than what it gives to that relationship. Many marriages and friendships fail because this is the type of love that people demonstrate. Only relationships that are built on God's love can truly flourish.

As humans, we often talk about showing love to others. We all say that all we need is love. Many of us believe we know what love is. In reality, however, we are only living by certain feelings that we call "love." Everyone wants to be loved, and most people want to love others in return. However, do we really know what love is? Real love is supernatural love. It is God's love in its most all-encompassing. God does not select only the beautiful people or the rich or the successful to love. He loves the world totally. His supernatural love is rooted in His fruit of the Spirit. Indeed, the ultimate fruit of the spirit is godlike love. It is also the ground from which spiritual fruit springs. When God's Spirit is at work in a person, amazing things happen. The person's whole life blossoms and bears beautiful fruit. And the most wonderful fruit of all is the giving and receiving of true love. Our human efforts alone can never produce godly love. But the good news is that we can have the divine type of love toward God and toward other people if we possess the indwelling of God's Spirit.

Paul wrote to the Galatians in the scripture in Galatians chapter 5, verses 22 and 23 (NIV) that "the fruit of the Spirit is love, joy, peace, long suffering, kindness, goodness, faithfulness, gentleness, self-control." Love tops the list because evidently, it is first in importance. It also encompasses all the other aspects of the fruit of the Spirit.

Love is a spirit. God has created us in His image, which means that we are created to love. We are created to need love, and we are created to give love. As people become more "world focused," they seem to develop a distorted view about what love truly is. The Bible, as already mentioned, tells us that "God is love," and the Bible also says that "God is Spirit." That means true love is a Spirit—the Holy Spirit. But of course, our world is filled with counterfeit forms of what people call love.

The fruit of the Holy Spirit describes true and authentic love. The first fruit of the Spirit is love, and all of the other fruits are characteristics of love. Love is more than a feeling, and it is more than an experience. It is the manifested presence of God—the glory of God. Since God is love, whenever we experience true love, we are also experiencing God's glorious presence. The second fruit is joy, so love is the ultimate joy that can be experienced. The third fruit listed is peace. Just as fear is a spirit, so is love a spirit of power and of peace. The other six fruits of the Spirit all have to do with actions of love and the power of love.

All of the fruits of the Spirit are the manifestations of the Holy Spirit, which is the manifestation of God's love in our own life. As we grow in intimate knowledge of the love of Christ, we are filled with all the fullness of God because Christ is the greatest revelation of God's love and the greatest manifestation of God's glory to man. Indeed, God is love, and he who abides in love abides in God and God in him. For many people, the world is a dark, lonely, and loveless place. As Christians, we have the answers people are longing for. We must let the glory of God's love shine through us to bring light and love to hurting people. Ultimately, however, what is of paramount importance is that we always remember that God loves us so much that He gave His Son in order that the world could be saved. Note that God's love is for everyone in the world, whoever believes in Him. We are to love others as God loves us. We are not to pick the nicest looking, most glamorous, or the most popular people to love. In fact, we are to love even our enemies. Jesus is our perfect example. As He was being crucified, He said, "Father, forgive them, for they know not what they do."

In the scripture in Romans chapter 8, verse 38 (NIV), Paul said, "For I am sure that neither death nor life, nor angels nor rulers, nor things present nor things to come, nor powers, nor height nor depth, nor anything else in all creation, will be able to separate us from the love of God in Christ Jesus our Lord." God's love is steadfast. God loves us whether we respond to Him in love or not. His love for us is not based on our response, but on His character. However, although God is love, this does not mean that we don't have any responsibility to respond to His love. What it means is that God is always ready to wrap us in His loving arms when we turn to Him in repentance and in faith. In contrast, worldly love is fickle. Those who claim they love us are there during the good times but keep their distance from us when the going gets rough. God will not leave us in the tough times. The promise of Jesus is: "I will never leave you nor forsake you" as it says in the scripture in Hebrews chapter 13, verse 5 (NIV).

So as an overview, we can see that while human love is self-ish and gain-based, God's love is sacrificial. While human love has strings attached and expects something in return, His love has no strings attached. Our love is conditional while His is unconditional. Our love gives, expecting something in return, while God's love gives simply to be a blessing. While our love can be easily offended and can be withdrawn when it is not appreciated or reciprocated, His love continues against all odds. In the case of our love, when we are disappointed, we can become totally discouraged. In the case of God's love, He may be disappointed, but He is never discouraged. Ultimately, we are sensual in love; He is spiritual in love. Human love is limited to our natural abilities, but with God's love we can surpass our human abilities.

In conclusion, our world now has an idea of love that is moving farther and farther away from the true love that is found only in God. It is a false imitation of the reality. The apostle Paul's description in 1 Corinthians chapter 13, verses 4 to 7 (NIV), remains the classic and concise picture of the true love that is God's love:

> Love is patient and kind; love does not envy or boast; it is not arrogant or rude. It does not insist on its own way; it is not irritable or resentful; it does not rejoice at wrongdoing, but rejoices with the truth. Love bears all things, believes all things, hopes all things, endures all things.

Indeed, God's supernatural love is His love covenant with us. And to Him be all the glory. Amen.

EPILOGUE

Liquid Love

And now these three remain: faith, hope and love.
But the greatest of these is love.
— 1 Corinthians 13:13 (NIV)

We have talked about every level of love, from its pureness to its obstruction, in this book. The reader will recall that the book opened with my memories of the traumatic past that threatened my very existence as a Christian, manifesting themselves as a malevolent attempt to destroy my love for and trust in others. They not only threatened my present, but my hope for a glorious future. My lack of forgiveness had replaced compassion, charity, and Christian accommodation, and in the process, having averted my face from God, He found it difficult to locate my face. This is why soul-searching can be so crucial in the life of a Christian. Because it was at that moment of realization, and in which I asked God to heal me, that I arrived at the revelation of the authentic nature of His love as the liquid current of ethereal energy that I have come to characterize as His liquid love coursed through my entire body. In squeezing my cold heart to allow His liquid love to pour out of me, all my fears dissolved into nothingness since He had taken me back to love. But something even greater happened. The surrender I had lost to distrust and mistrust because of the hurt I had suffered at the hands of others now came back since in experiencing the liquid love of God, I could also sincerely ask for my surrender back from God Himself, and I was now ushered into my new place of intimacy with God—a place filled with nothing but love, trust, and hope. That entire surreal experience provided the motivation for the book you now hold in your hands. If you are someone whose love has been betrayed, causing you to enter into a life of distrust and mistrust, this experience of surrender will be your own story of liberation too in Jesus's name.

The next question now becomes how to shake off the garbage that others have heaped on you in the form of rejection and low self-esteem, which makes you believe that you are not worthy of love. You will recall that we discussed that this rejection comes from what you perceive to be the high expectations others have of you, which in turn makes you think you have to be perfect to be loved. As we have seen, this is not only unrealistic, but impossible, as perfection belongs only to God. The only way out of this quagmire is to forgive yourself and forgive others. Yes, forgiveness is easier pronounced than done. But then, the walk of love is not an easy one, and it comes with tremendous personal sacrifice. To love is to expend effort. Each time we choose to love unconditionally, it will cost something. Nothing that is truly noble comes without some sacrifice. And forgiveness is not only noble, but the true path to healing. Indeed, you must forgive yourself for every act of indiscretion you have committed. You must forgive those who hurt you and just let it go. Enter into your kingdom of inner peace by forgiving yourself freely, and the only way to do this is by getting rid of those feelings and thoughts that hold you from loving others and loving yourself freely. Should the sacrifice of love become so tough for us, God has already set us an example by the way He loves. He loves us by giving, by serving, and by sacrificing. God's love for us is universal and unconditional as is evident in its accessibility and in its separation from our moral or spiritual status.

Another important lesson that this book teaches is that even though things may not necessarily turn out as we would wish, our mouth can still be filled with songs of praise to our Lord. Only a healthy spiritual heart, and that is a heart that reflects God's unconditional love, can remain in a consistent state of gratitude to God. Conversely, it is only when our heart is spiritually healthy that we can have assurance of a healthy physical heart. To fully appreciate the wonders of God in our daily experiences is to develop a healthy heart of love, and without this, our physical heart goes into decay.

We also learned about the very pervasive tendency of offense to strike at the very root of a believer's faith and its propensity to rob one of the peace of mind that is so necessary to worship God in truth and in spirit. What this translates to is that if you do not make deliberate effort to separate yourself from perceived offense, because in truth, it's all about perception, you soon start to separate yourself from the love of God. Yet the sad thing about perception is that it is based on the deception that allows us only to see issues from the selfish and self-centeredness that can only result in mutual conflict. Fortunately, we have available to us a tool that can counteract the effect of faulty perception in separating us from the unconditional love of God, and that is mindfulness about the things of God. The more we insist on occupying our mind space with thoughts of the love of God, the more we disallow offense from creating thoughts that will detract us from our love walk with God and from our destiny.

Another important phase in our love journey is that place of pain where we were stuck in the first place. We must go back and restart our journey from that place of pain. The crucial question, however, is why you have to retrace your steps back to that place where you were originally stuck. The reason is simple. There is something at that place of pain that must come into your prized possession before you can make further progress in your love walk with God. That thing you must possess is your freedom. And that freedom lies in the power of forgiveness. Indeed, it is in practicing total and unconditional forgiveness that you can obtain this freedom and make progress. Should you insist on moving along without forgiveness, you will find yourself consumed by that lack, and your future will offer nothing but a life filled with pain and disappointment. Part of the dilemma you will face is a need to blame someone for your woes. You may even find yourself blaming God. And you may be right. The only thing wrong is that you may not know why you are right. You would be right because God has a purpose for allowing your hurt. He is neither wasting your time nor is He wasting His. He has a purpose. He always has a purpose. God's ultimate purpose is to use that hurt and disappointment to bring you into a place of authentic wealth. And that is why you're being left with only one viable option and one path. You have to take this one path. And that is the path of trust. You have to trust in God's love for He is always at work in you, and this is because He loves you anyway.

The next phase in your journey is a place of rest. In your love walk with God, there are two very important places where you can find rest with Him. The two places are the resting place of victory and the resting place of faith. To be victorious means to be triumphant in battle. To make substantial progress in your quest to defeat Satan, you need a defensive strategy. Our problem is that we put our hands up and try to defend ourselves against the enemy. We need aggression at the front line of battle. Paul teaches us in scripture that we are engaged in a spiritual warfare against the rulers and principalities who govern the world of darkness, and that we have the weapons with which we must fight. These weapons are six in number: the Word of God, praise and worship, pleading the blood of Jesus, prayer, the word of our testimony, and the name of Jesus.

The second place of rest is that of faith. However, this rest is a rest in service because it is also coupled with a yoke for activity. That means, inherent in your confidence of a rest in faith is an active and vibrant participation in your walk of love with God. As a Christian, you will never find rest in idleness. There is no unrest greater than that of the sluggard, and for you to lay claim to your rest, you have to take Christ's yoke and be actively engaged in His service.

We all seem to be sailing on a boat whose floor is lined with broken pieces. These broken pieces are our: broken marriages, broken health, broken finances, broken dreams and visions, and broken relationships. We need three weapons for the restoration of our broken lives. These are the three weapons we need to become a receiver of the liquid love of God. They are humility, giving, and love.

At a crucial point on our love journey, we will have to sit down and calmly gaze deep into our soul to confront the ugliest traits that are holding us back from experiencing the coursing of the liquid love of God through our being. For most of us, these traits will include: bitterness, hurt, pain, rejection, loneliness, jealousy, betrayal, anger, and unforgiveness. It is also at this point that we will have to respond to the inevitable question of whether we truly love God, or whether we love those things that are eating away at us more than we love God. We cannot love God yet hold those ugly works in our heart. We cannot truly love God while harboring a spirit of unforgiveness. We cannot love God purely while holding onto anger and bitterness. When we can love God more than these, then we are loving God.

In essence, love and bitterness cannot coexist in the life of a child of God. Love and unforgiveness cannot dwell in the same place. Love and hatred cannot operate in the same environment. Resentment will have to vacate our inner space so that the unconditional emotion that is the unadulterated liquid love of God can take residence, for truly, as Jesus says in the book of Luke, you cannot serve two masters. It is either you will hate the one and love the other, or you will be devoted to the one and despise the other. Period. This is how it works. When that space in you that is supposed to be occupied by love is occupied by unforgiveness, unforgiveness starts to grow to occupy that space, and, in the process, it gradually forces love out. The truth is that nature does not like a vacuum. Nature demands that every space be filled with something, and the same principle operates in our spiritual lives. If our inner space is not filled with love, we leave room for its occupation by the killers of our soul, like anger, resentment, and unforgiveness. The irony, though, is that even if we rid ourselves of these negative emotions and do not immediately start to replace them with thoughts of love, we are still leaving space for occupation by unwholesome emotions.

One of the greatest antagonists to our experience of the love of God is mortal grief. Grief, as an emotion of intense sorrow, can be particularly deep, especially when it is for a dearly beloved person. Almost invariably, it is the price we pay for the very close bond we have for another. That is why nothing is as painful as losing one's own child. But becoming a believer is supposed to endow us with the strength to handle grief. This is because while God expects us to grieve, we are however expected to do so as people who have been given a certain hope in heaven, as He says we are blessed as we mourn for we shall be comforted. Certain facts are unassailable. From the day we make our entrance into this world, our irrevocable destiny is to die. Fact. It is an unavoidable destiny. Fact. From dust we came, and to dust we must and will return. Fact. In that case, given the inevitability of passage, how should we grieve? There is a human response to grief, and there is a divine response. At the human end of the spectrum, the only hope available to us in times of dark despair is that "it will pass." Indeed, it will. This too shall pass. We will somehow reach, not the end of hurting itself, but, thankfully, the end of the unbearable side to the hurt. The divine response to our grief is simply to be grateful to God. We have to trust Him that His love for us transcends whatever agony we are experiencing. Ultimately, our obligation is to trust that God's love for us is much deeper than the pain we are experiencing.

In this book, we also learn that pride is one of the greatest impediments to a genuine love walk with God, and He knows it only too well. That is why God said He will give us a crown of beauty for our pain. The condition, however, that He gives is that we first have to take off our crown of pride so as to create space on our head for His crown of love. That crown is one of beauty, and its precious stones are the elements of the fruit of the spirit: love, joy, long-suffering, gentleness, goodness, meekness, temperance, and faith.

Perfect order is the stuff of which God's equally perfect timing is made. That is why patience is such an enduring virtue in the life of a true believer. When you have allowed patience to have its way, and to complete its work within you, the issue of struggle in any form no longer arises. The reason why some have to struggle so much in life and in ministry, is that they did not allow patience to accomplish its "perfect work in them." Put succinctly, there are steps that we simply cannot afford to skip on this glorious journey to a place of unconditional love. The very real transformation that must take place in our life to arrive at God's sanctuary of love is not possible if we avoid a season or phase in our life, for truly, to everything there is a season and a time to every purpose under heaven. We cannot skip the necessary steps. To love God is to trust Him and to have faith that, in due season, we shall reap the fruits of our labor in His vineyard.

It is in the tragedy that is the contemporary lot of mankind that we must seek a purpose for God's love. These are perilous times in which people are living lives of trepidation and quiet desperation. Worse, we all seem to be great civil engineers. The only tragedy in this fact is that we continually employ our engineering skills to erect walls of discord, disharmony, and disenchantment between ourselves. Where is the hope for mankind in all these? Only love can put a halt to our global tragedy. The only hope for mankind is love. What the world needs is love. We must all commit to building bridges of love between one another's hearts. That is why love is the greatest challenge for humanity as a whole. We each have an individual, and a collective mission. That mission is to continue to spread this love. Indeed, the world, now more than ever, needs to feel and see the unconditional love of God as its only hope. Therein lies the purpose for the enduring love that He has put in place to nourish us and to give us hope for a greater tomorrow. Yet we must fight for this love. We must fight for it in our marriages, in our schools, and in our churches. True love is rarely found on the surface of life. We must earnestly pursue it in the subterranean depths of the human condition, and it is in the finding of it that we will also discover the purpose for it.

In many respects, we are all prodigals. In our quest to chart unexplored territories, we seem to forget that freedom is not necessarily doing what we want, but what we ought. Yet no matter how far gone we are, Jesus is always waiting to receive us with open arms. Painful, also, as our errant journeys of exploration may turn out, they are not wasted enterprises of discovery. God tends to use every part of such indiscretions to teach us His precepts and to show us how to comfort someone else who went astray. And that is why, no matter how far we have veered off course, the unconditional love of God wants us back, and His arms are always wide open to receive us. It is also in this enduring patience of God with us that we can arrive at the difference between our mortal love and His supernatural love. The love of man is natural, and it is mercurial, being subject to mood, change, and circumstances. This makes the love of man limited, both in expression and in scope. The love of God, on the other hand, is supernatural and, being totally divine, can only be shared by the Spirit of the Lord. But then, this is not surprising, for "God, Himself, is love." Therefore, when all is said and done, God is love and love is God.

So much for the basic knowledge that this book has placed at our disposal. However, knowledge acquisition in itself quickly turns into an exercise in futility if that knowledge is not employed to take us to another level. Put in other words, knowledge must find a way to transpose itself into wisdom for wisdom is nothing if not knowledge in application. It therefore now becomes our burden to determine what we will productively do with the knowledge gleaned from this book.

Your life has been set in a pattern designed and destined by God. That is why, outside of the will of God, you will lose direction and purpose. This is also why many find themselves floundering in certain areas or aspects of their lives for years. We find a perfect example of this sort of human dysfunction in the children of Israel. It took them forty years to arrive at Canaan, the Promised Land, and we know that, even at that, many of them could not go into Canaan because of their unbelief or doubt in God. Yet this was a journey that would have geometrically taken only eleven days! After all, the laws of physics teach us that the shortest distance between two points is a simple straight line. Indeed, while the initial directions we were furnished with for our journey may appear straightforward enough, we are often rerouted, or perhaps more accurately put, "recalculated," to adapt to external and unanticipated extraneous factors such as destiny, loss of a job, weather conditions, college expenses, movement to a new house, illness, or even divorce.

As we relate it to our personal journey today, we may have the tendency to fall into the temptation of thinking that the shorter route is the best route, and therefore attempt to reroute ourselves to accommodate our propensity for "the easy, the fast, and the convenient." I recall once having a vision a few years ago before commencing my PhD studies. I was walking along a road, all by myself, when a car pulled up beside me. It was a small car, looking somewhat like a Volkswagen, and its top was down for it was a convertible. The occupants of the car were people I was familiar with from my former church. The driver yelled at me, "Do you want a ride?" and I quickly responded, "No, thank you. I would rather walk" with a smile on my face. They took off, and I kept walking along the road. Shortly after that encounter, I arrived at the foot of a bridge. It was a very long bridge. As I stopped to look across the bridge, in the distance, I could see the car up ahead moving along on the bridge. I said out loud to myself, as I stood at the foot of the bridge, watching them driving fast across the bridge, "I should have taken that ride." Soon after, I woke up.

I can say without equivocation, that now, a few years down the line, many of those people in the car had completed their educational goals while it took me several years after this to obtain my Ph.D. Naturally, I could come to quite a few interesting conclusions; however, I will leave it at just the salient knowledge God has never permitted me to take a shortcut in any field of endeavor. I have always had to work hard and long to achieve my set goals. Frankly, I don't know if I am just a "hard head" and need a lot of work or if God is digging deep within me to build me up "tall" or if it's a combination of both.

The scripture in Exodus chapter 13, verses 17 and 18 (NIV), says, "When Pharaoh let the people go, God did not lead them by way of the Philistines, although it was nearer; for God said, 'The people may have a change of heart when they see war, and return to Egypt.' So, God led the people roundabout, by way of the wilderness at the Sea of Reeds."

Contemporary Bible scholar Avivah Zornberg notes,

> The opposition of the road not taken (the "straight" road) to the route chosen (the "crooked" route) carries its own paradoxical resonance. Obviously, the straight road is preferable to the "crooked"; strategically, physically, and ethically; indeed, the metaphorical use of these expressions—the straight and the crooked paths—is commonplace in ethical writings. Yet,

here, the Torah makes a point of God's not taking the obvious route... Through this opening
speech at the moment of redemption, we understand that the Israelites, even at this moment, are
ambivalent about the movement to freedom.

What we can infer from the seminal analysis of this eminent
scholar is that there is a very real struggle that you may be facing:
a reluctance to try something new to veer off the beaten path into
uncharted territory or to leave your comfort zone, as it were. After
all, why would your senses lead you to take the risk of traveling a path
that is less familiar, or perhaps even less comfortable, all by yourself,
and on your own? Fear is more likely to immobilize you with its own
capacity to torment you. Faith mobilizes. Faith works by love.

In his classic poem "The Road Not Taken," Robert Frost wrote,
"Two roads diverged in a wood, and I—I took the one less traveled
by, and that has made all the difference." Love has no fear. We resist
change because we fear we can't handle it, or most significantly, we
feel that we may not be able to control what the change may bring.

Coming full circle to contemporary events, when I first heard
the news of the heartless killings of children and adults at the high
school in Parkland, Florida, my heart broke into a million pieces.
I immediately started praying for the families, but I simply could
not get them out of my spirit. The next day, I was driving into
Philadelphia from New Jersey when the thought of those children
came to my mind again. I started crying. Yet all of a sudden, a shift
occurred in my heart and in my psyche. I reflected on the goodness
of the Lord and how He has been so gracious and so merciful to me.
I thought back to my husband, and I recalled the great husband and
father he once was. I thought about how confident I had been in his
love for his family. He had always been a great family man, but he
suffered a great loss some years back, and something shifted inside
of him. Suddenly, he transformed into a man I could no longer recognize. Even our children felt there was something clearly different
about their father. I thought about that Christmas time when all
of the family were together, as is our tradition, and he pulled out

a beautiful short black suede jacket with a fox collar and gave it to me for a Christmas gift. I was so excited and grateful for it. Then he brought out another beautiful box…then another beautiful box…then another…then another… and finally, another beautiful box with a coat in it. I have always loved coats. He bought me six beautiful coats that Christmas. It isn't just the coats that I want to draw attention to, but that it was the kind of thing he would do to add that special touch to our relationship and to show me that he cared about me in a very special way. I thought about how, for years, he would buy all five of our daughters' teddy bears, candies, and flowers on Valentine's Day, and make a production out of it all. Then that thing happened. And it threw him totally off course. He became cold, callous, and critical. Yet we knew he still loved his family. We were and would always remain the pride of his life.

So as I drove down the highway with tears streaming down my face, I realized, "I miss my husband." Later that day, I texted my husband that message, and something in him shifted. I knew he was feeling unloved and unappreciated, and that little text was enough to let him know I was still here for him. That text message actually meant, "I still love you. We can work out any issues we have together. I know you are a great man, and something is amiss. I want to understand." Now the healing could begin.

Yes, something broke in us. This happened because I allowed love to dominate and to change my own perspective. Life is too short and too precious for us to allow it to take a journey all on its own. We must insist on taking firm control of the steering wheel of life. Redirect your life through love, and let love be the driving force of your life. And then, I arrived at yet another reality: our love is continually tested. We think we have been touched once with God's finger of love and we are all right. But God touches us again and again with His finger of love, beckoning to us again and again to come up higher and deeper in His love. His liquid love peels off layers and layers of love, meaning, you can't put a measure to His love. You can't reach a place at which you believe you have all the love you need. You can't be so narcissistic to believe that the love you have for someone is all the love there is to give. But when you let God's liquid love touch you in your broken places, you will learn that God's love has no cap to it since it is endless, and life is good.

Love makes the world go round. This is a very true adage. Sadly, the times are not only dangerous, but actually perilous. These are times of extreme selfishness and self-centeredness. They are times when people are only interested in aggrandizing themselves and celebrating themselves on a pedestal of ego and pride in the process relegating love to an obscure background. Sadly, the consequence of all these is that love appears to be fast becoming both outdated and antiquated and whose very conception has also become totally bewildering to most people. This is not surprising.

The opposite of love is hate. The new wave of hate has destroyed the value of human life, and it has inexorably caused the world to move away from conduct that demonstrates respect and integrity. These were the attributes that made the world great.

Dr. Martin Luther King put it succinctly when he said, "Darkness cannot drive out darkness; only light can." By the same token, hatred cannot drive out hatred; only love can. Matt Redman, in his song "Gracefully Broken," croons, "Here I am God, arms wide open, pouring out my life, gracefully broken." Indeed, we need to get away from our own selfish and personal needs and stop thinking in egocentric terms and open up our arms and our minds to global partnerships that will allow to gloriously explore the world of love.

The truth is that love possesses its own worth in self-cost. This is because love loves at its own detriment. Yet this is the liquid love that is "pure" love. It is love that is not tainted, has no pollutants, and has no bacteria growing therein. It is love that is not laced with anything else. Certainly, it has not been treated with anything and simply looks like what it is: love. Liquid love is God's own pure love, and that is why it is able to burn off anything that offends it.

At this emotionally exhausting point, dear reader, my sincere prayer for you is that you will allow the special grace of God's liquid love to melt away the poison from your life so that you will arrive at that special freedom that will allow you to walk unfettered in the fullness of life. Furthermore, my prayer is that you will allow God's love to totally melt any coldness you may have in your heart so you can have a completely feeling heart all over again. God's love will melt any and all indifference in your heart so that you can take up a worthy cause all over again. God's love will melt your disappointed heart so that you can be filled with hope for a glorious future all over again. Finally, my fervent prayer is that God has used this book to deposit an eternal measure of His love into your heart, and from you, into the hearts of many needy others. To Him be the eternal glory. Amen.

ABOUT THE AUTHOR

Rena' was ordained on February 18, 2000, by the renowned Dr. Evelyn Graves of Christ Chapel Church in Yeadon, Pennsylvania, where she and her family were active members for over twenty-five years. Under the direction of the Holy Spirit and her husband, Reggie, their five daughters, and their families, all moved their membership in 2005 to Sharon Baptist Church in Philadelphia under the astute leadership of Bishop Keith Reed, Sr. where Rena' is an associate minister, and Shepherd for both of the Care Cell and Intercessory Prayer Ministries.

Rena' D. Morrow, PhD is the founder of Gracious Women's Fellowship, a ministry that is a midwife to women to help them birth their God given vision and divine purpose in our Lord and Savior Jesus Christ. She believes every believer should walk in the highest integrity—the Gospel of Jesus Christ, who is the final authority. She is also a certified edutherapist through Rational Emotive Spiritual Therapy taking trouble souls to the truth within.

Dr. Morrow has an extensive educational background. She attended several bible schools including the Philadelphia Biblical University where she earned certification in pastoral counseling.

Dr. Morrow was a Distinguished Educator for the Pennsylvania Department of Education building capacity for distressed school districts. She earned her master's degree from Antioch University in elementary education and an administrative certification from Cheyney University. Rena' holds a Pennsylvania Superintendent Letter of Eligibility from Eastern University and a PhD in Organizational Leadership with an emphasis in education, also from Eastern University.

Her passion is to revenge ignorance on both an academic and spiritual level through the simple preaching and teaching of the "truth." Her philosophy is found in John 8:32 (NIV):

> And ye shall know the truth, and the truth shall make you free.

Armored with a mission from her Lord and Savior Jesus Christ found in Isaiah 61:1–5 is the impetus to the work that she does and loves.

Rena' D. Morrow, PhD and her husband, Reggie, have been married for over 40 years and have 5 daughters, Michelle, Ingrid, L'Tanya, Jasmine, and Morgan. Three sons-in-law, Darren, Kelvin, Gordon, and one son-in-law to be Devon, and 5 grandchildren Kelsii, Chloe, Destiny, Donte, Zoe, and baby Winter is on her way. Her family is the love of her life.

9 781098 041144